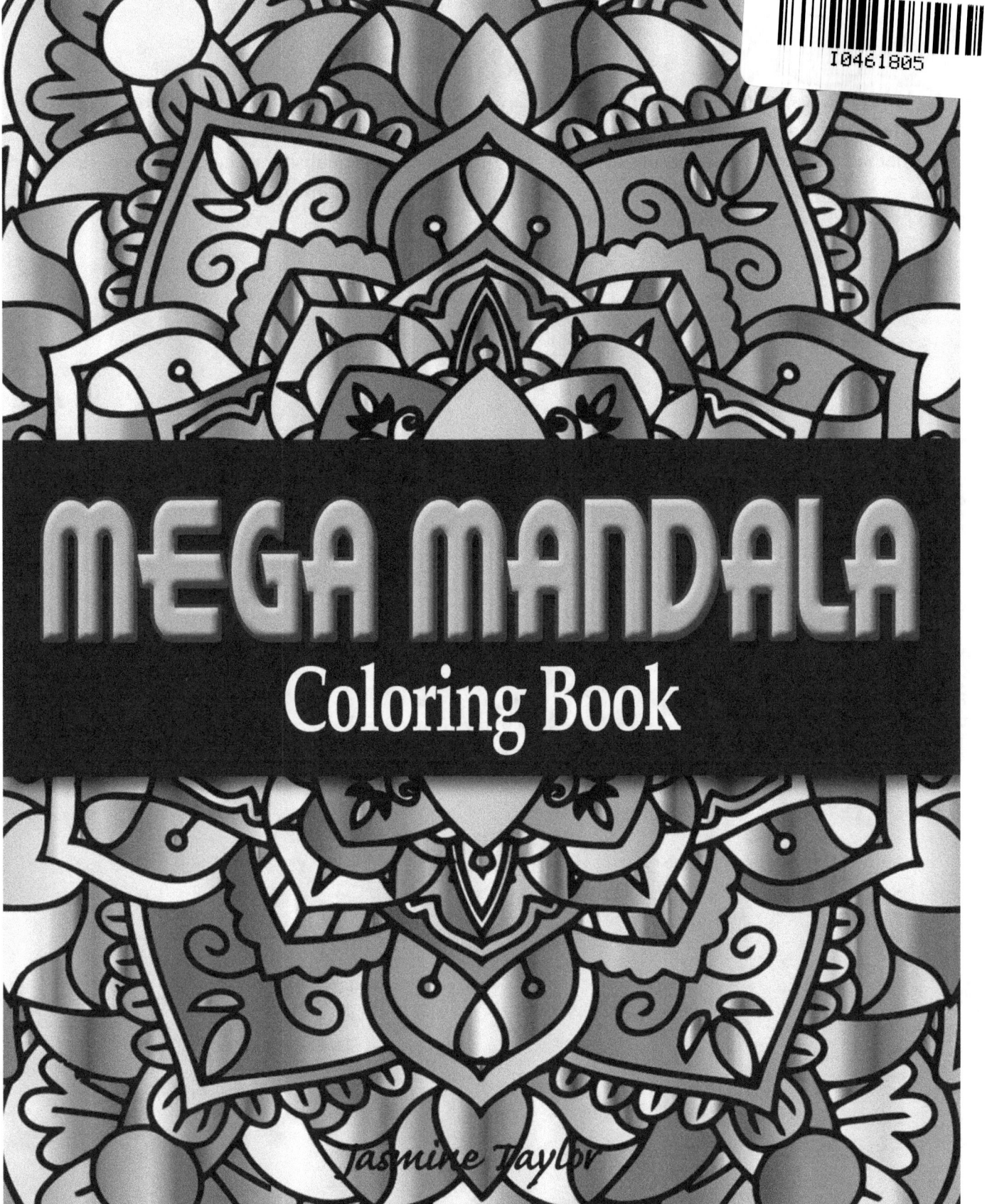

MEGA MANDALA
Coloring Book

Jasmine Taylor

I0461805

Copyright © 2019 by Jasmine Taylor

Book design by Jasmine Taylor

All rights reserved. No part of this book may be reproduced, distributed or transmitted in any form or by any means including photocopying, recording, or other electronic or mechanical methods, without prior permission in writing from the author/publisher. The only exception is by a reviewer, who may quote short excerpts in a review.

ISBN 978-0-359-87258-9

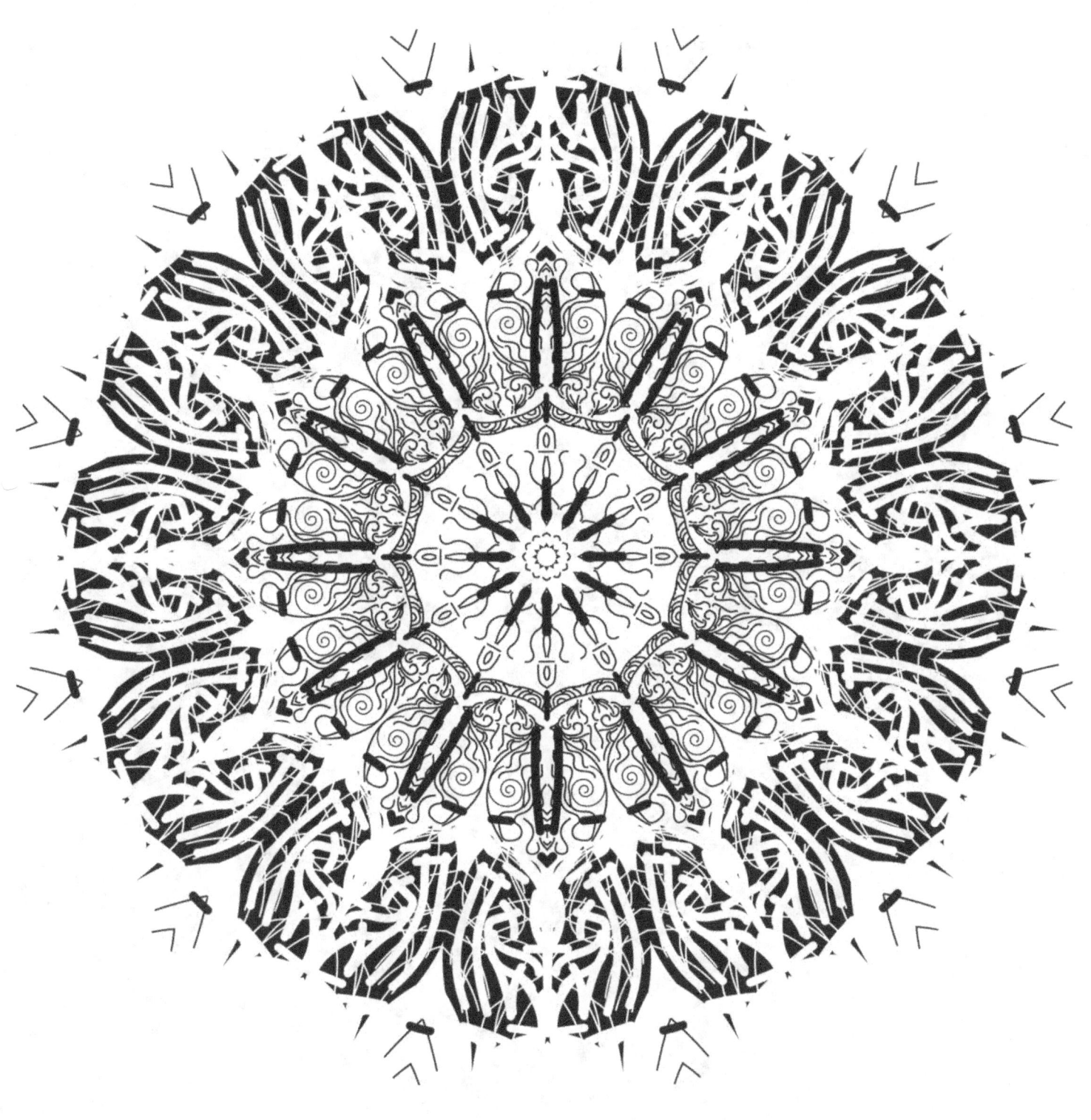

ARTIST

_____

NAME

_____

DATE

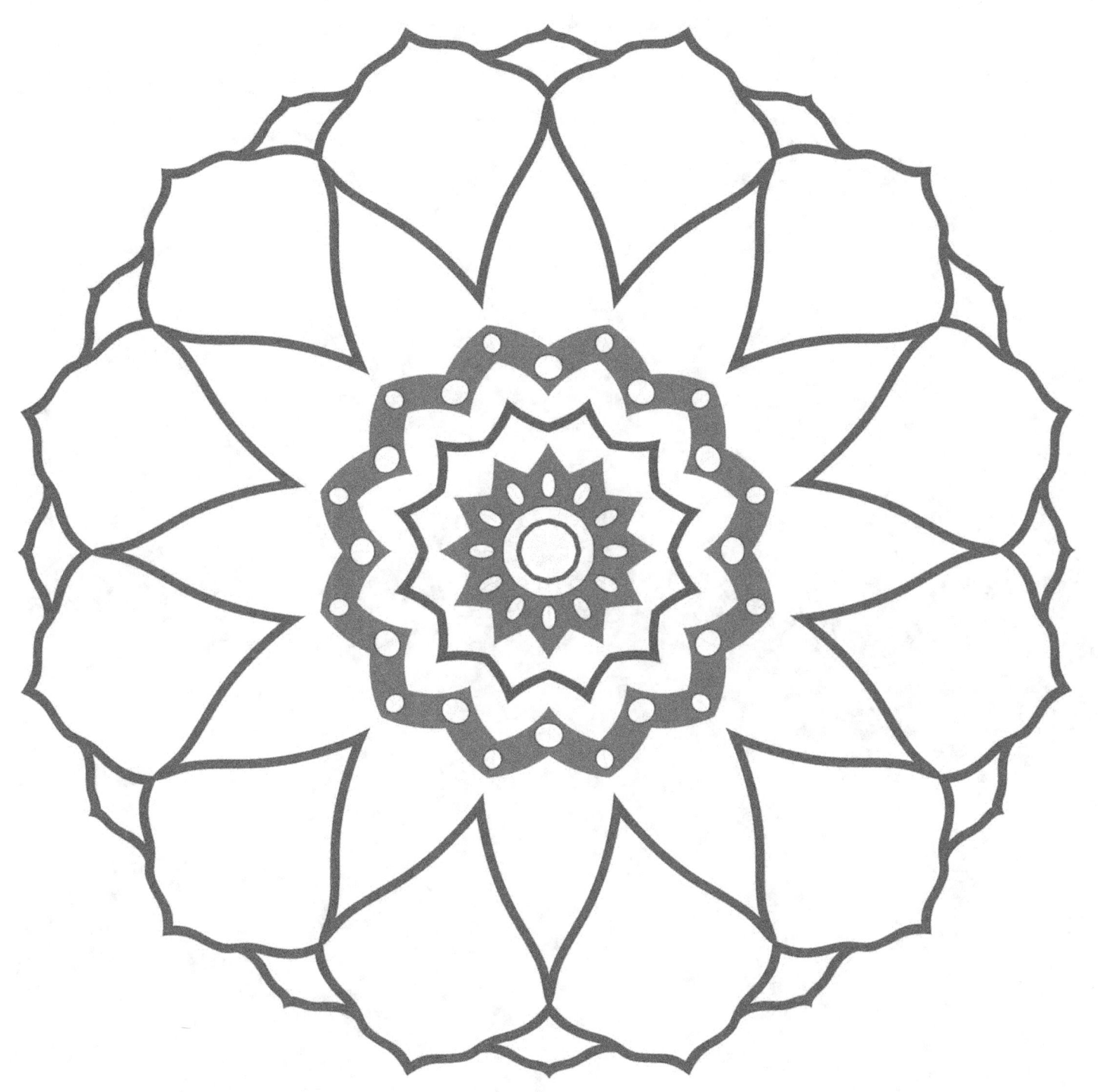

ARTIST

_____

NAME

_____

DATE

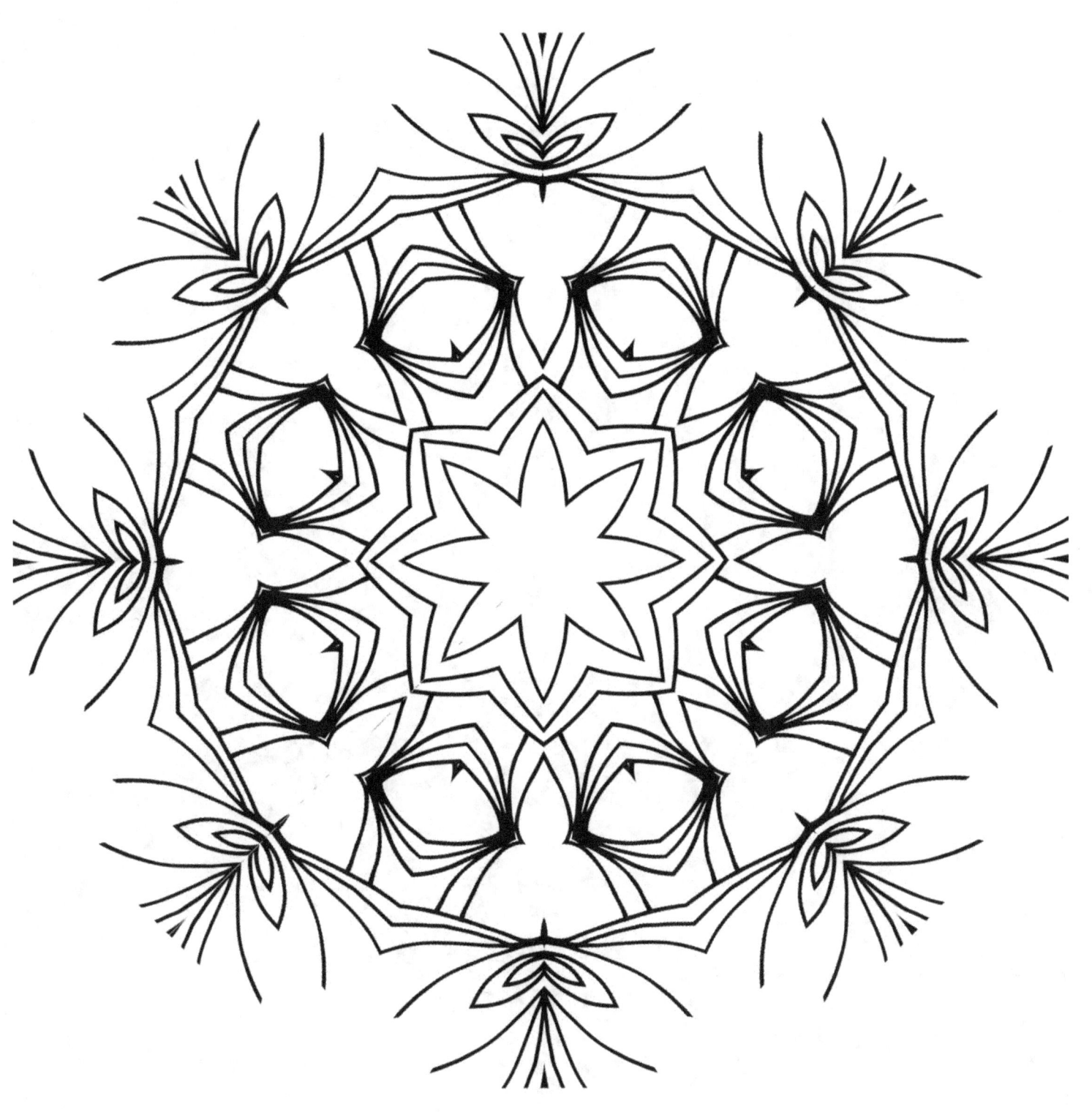

A R T I S T

_____

NAME

_____

DATE

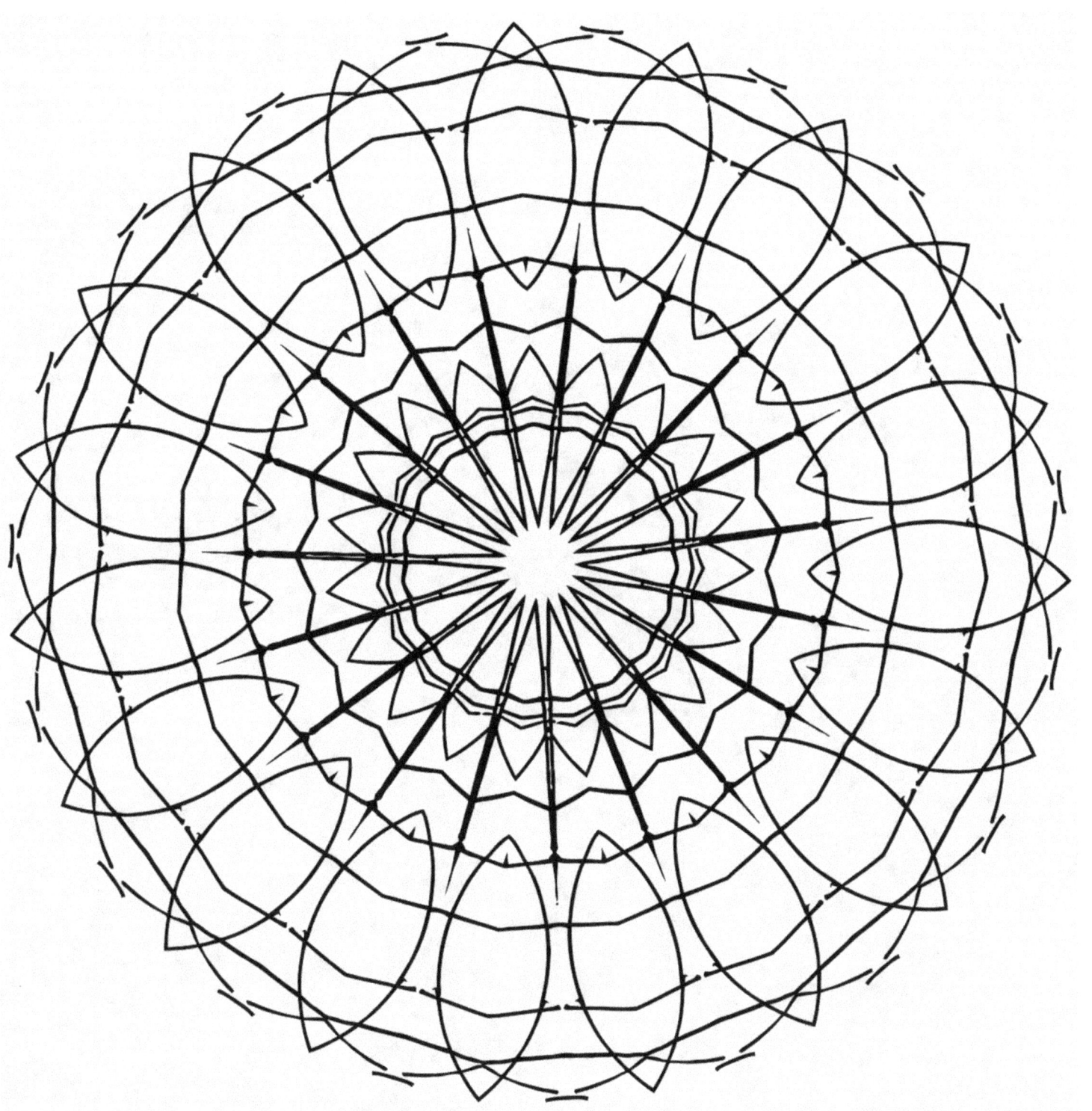

A R T I S T

_____

NAME

_____

DATE

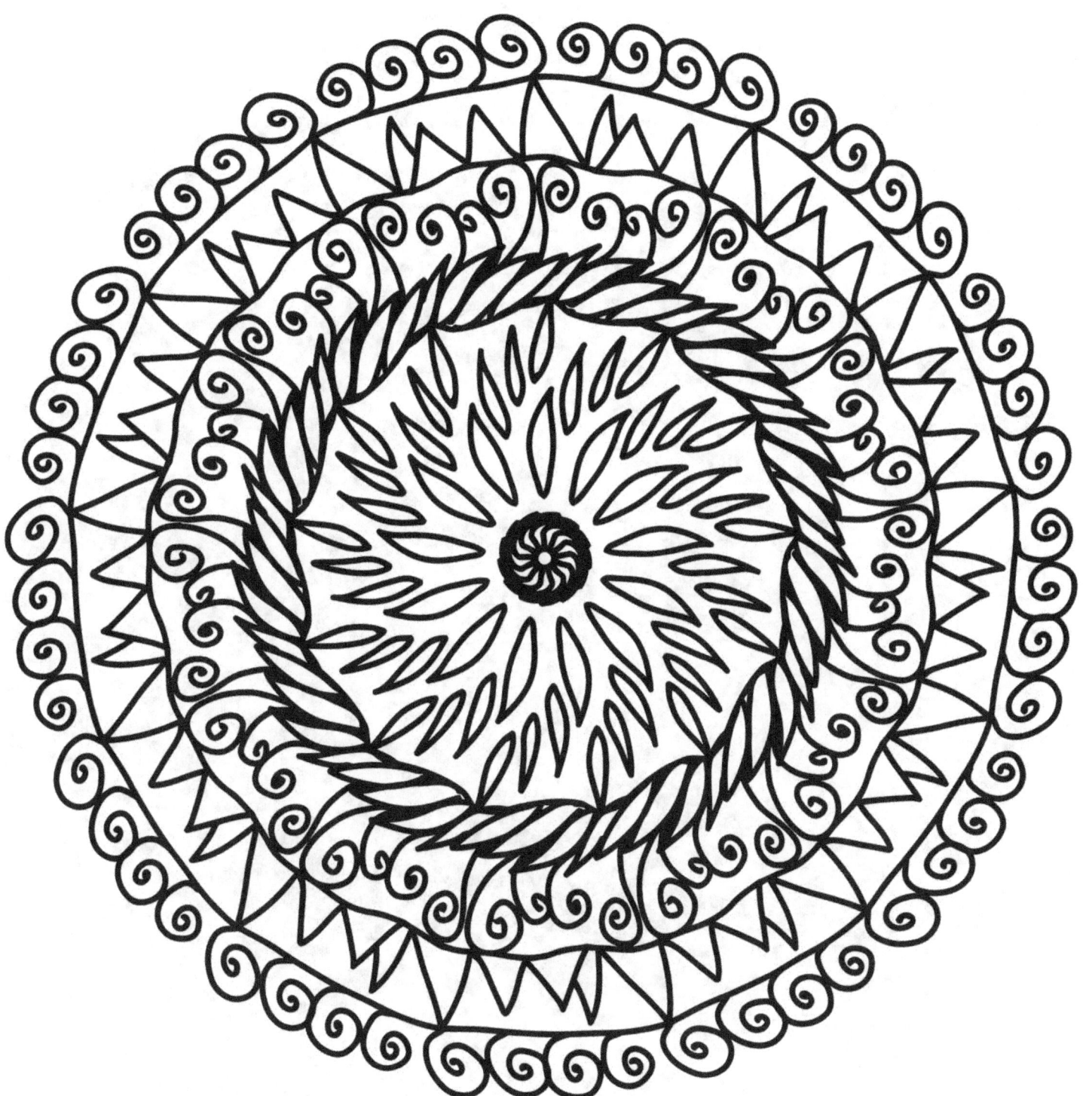

ARTIST

NAME

DATE

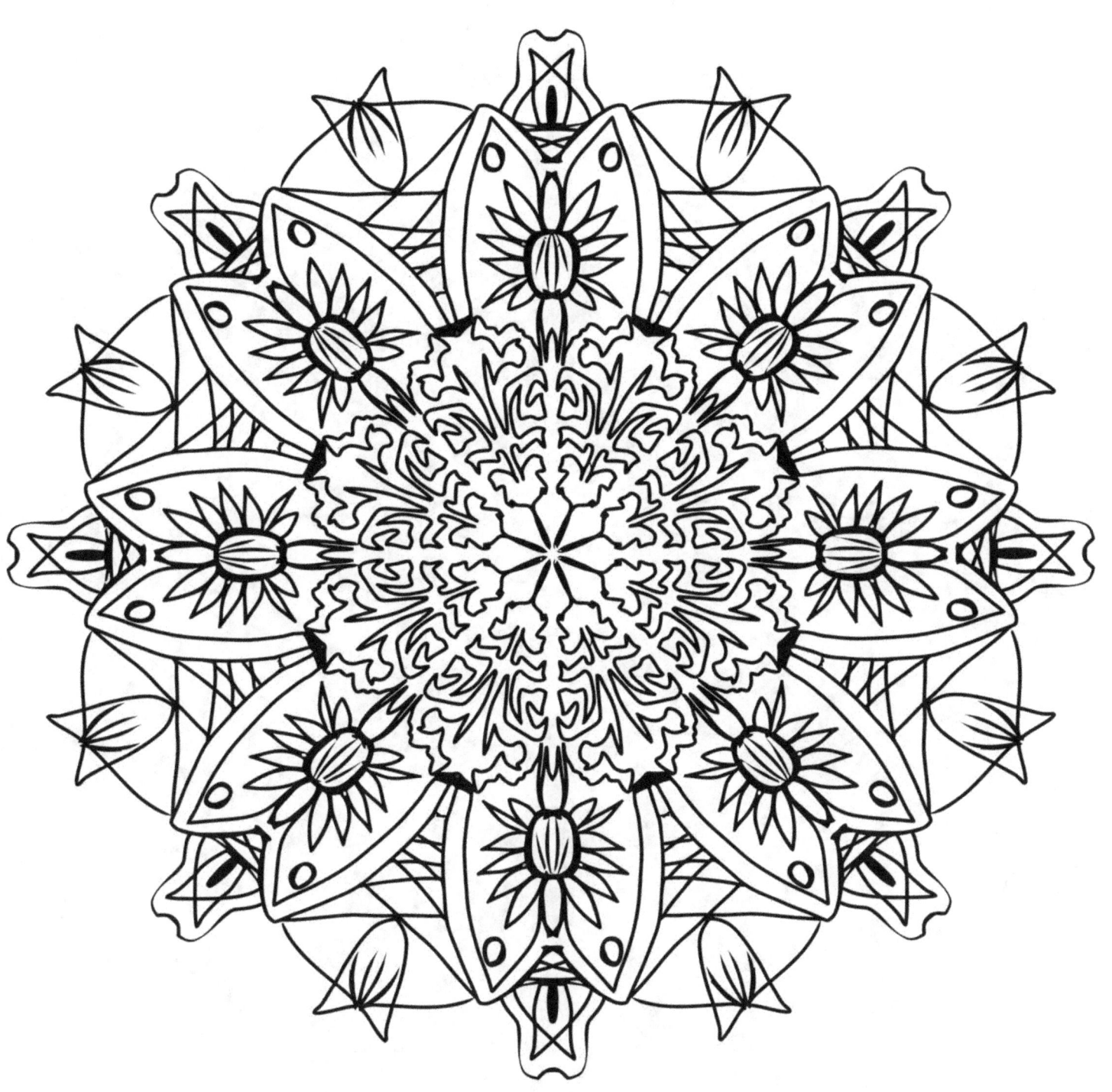

ARTIST

_____

NAME

_____

DATE

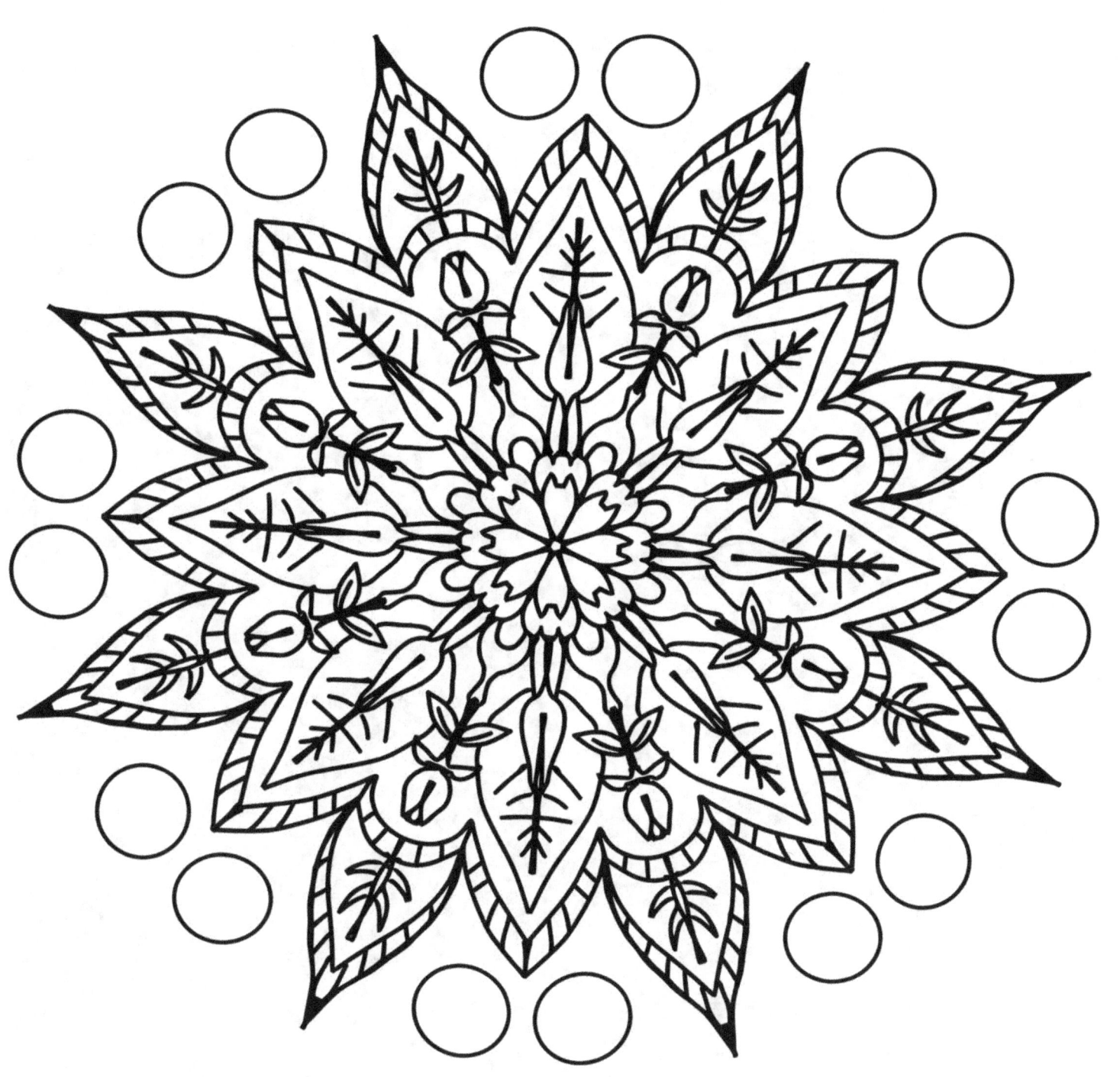

ARTIST

_____

NAME

_____

DATE

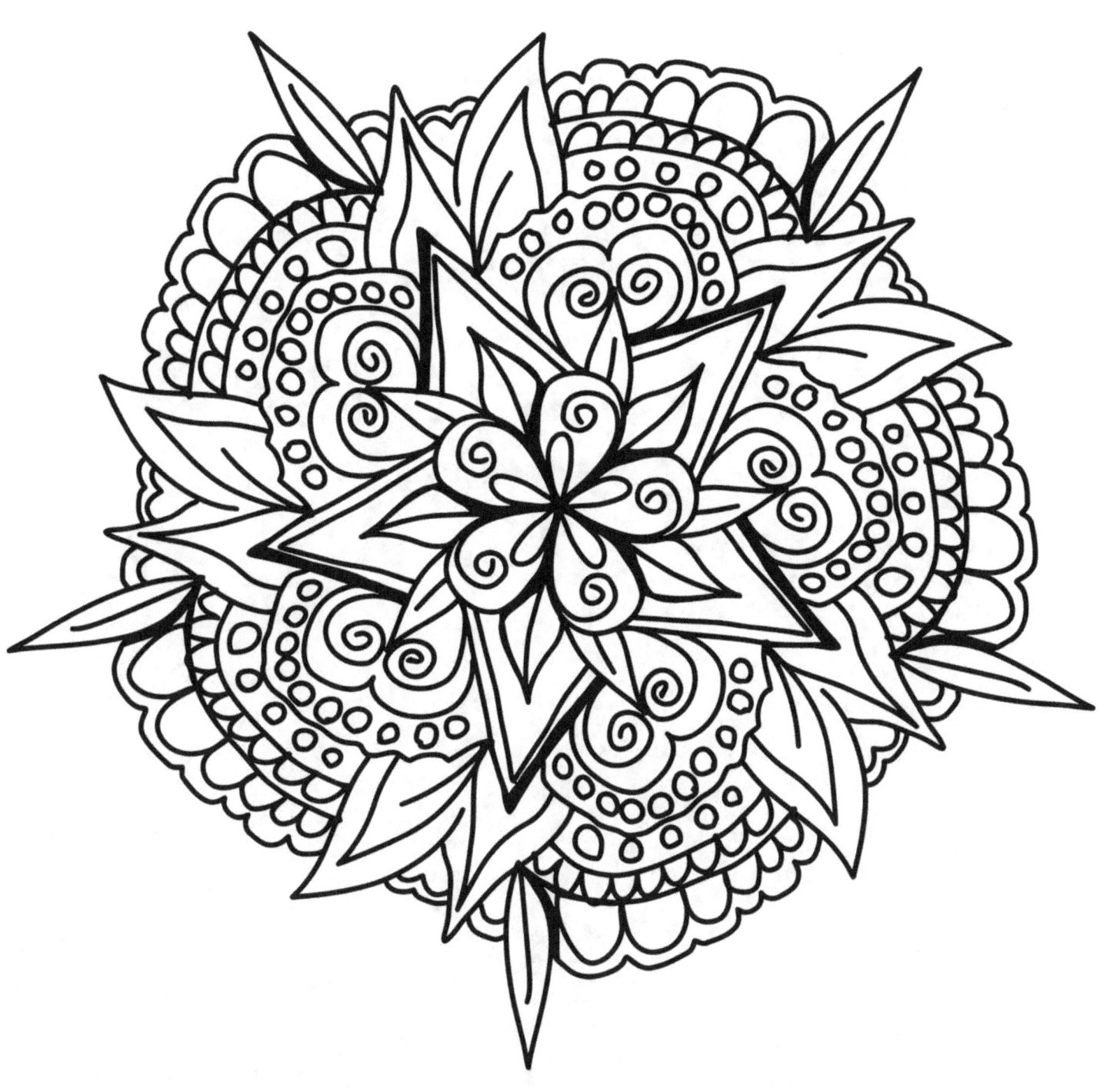

A R T I S T

_____
NAME

_____
DATE

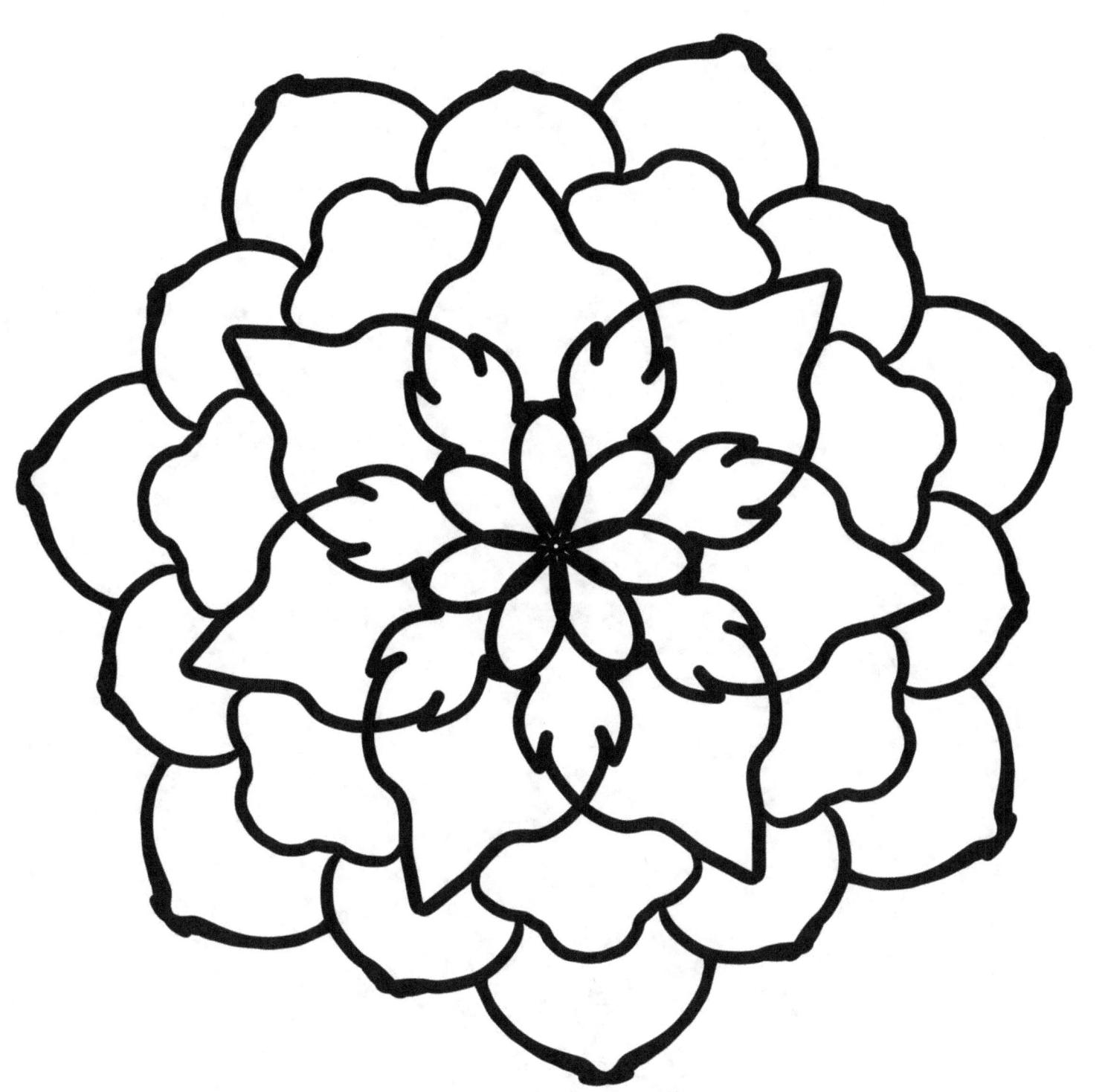

ARTIST

_____

NAME

_____

DATE

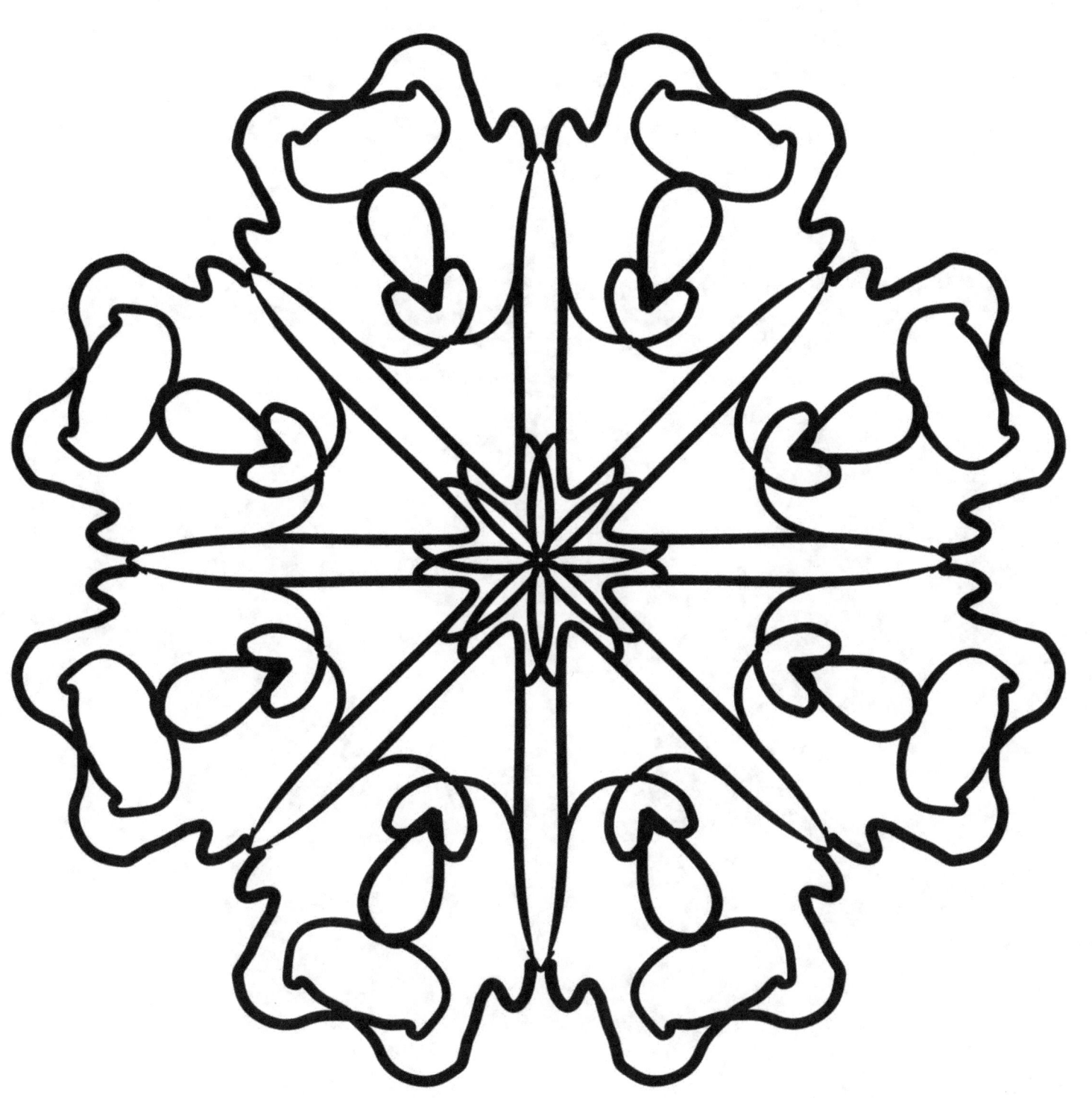

ARTIST

_____

NAME

_____

DATE

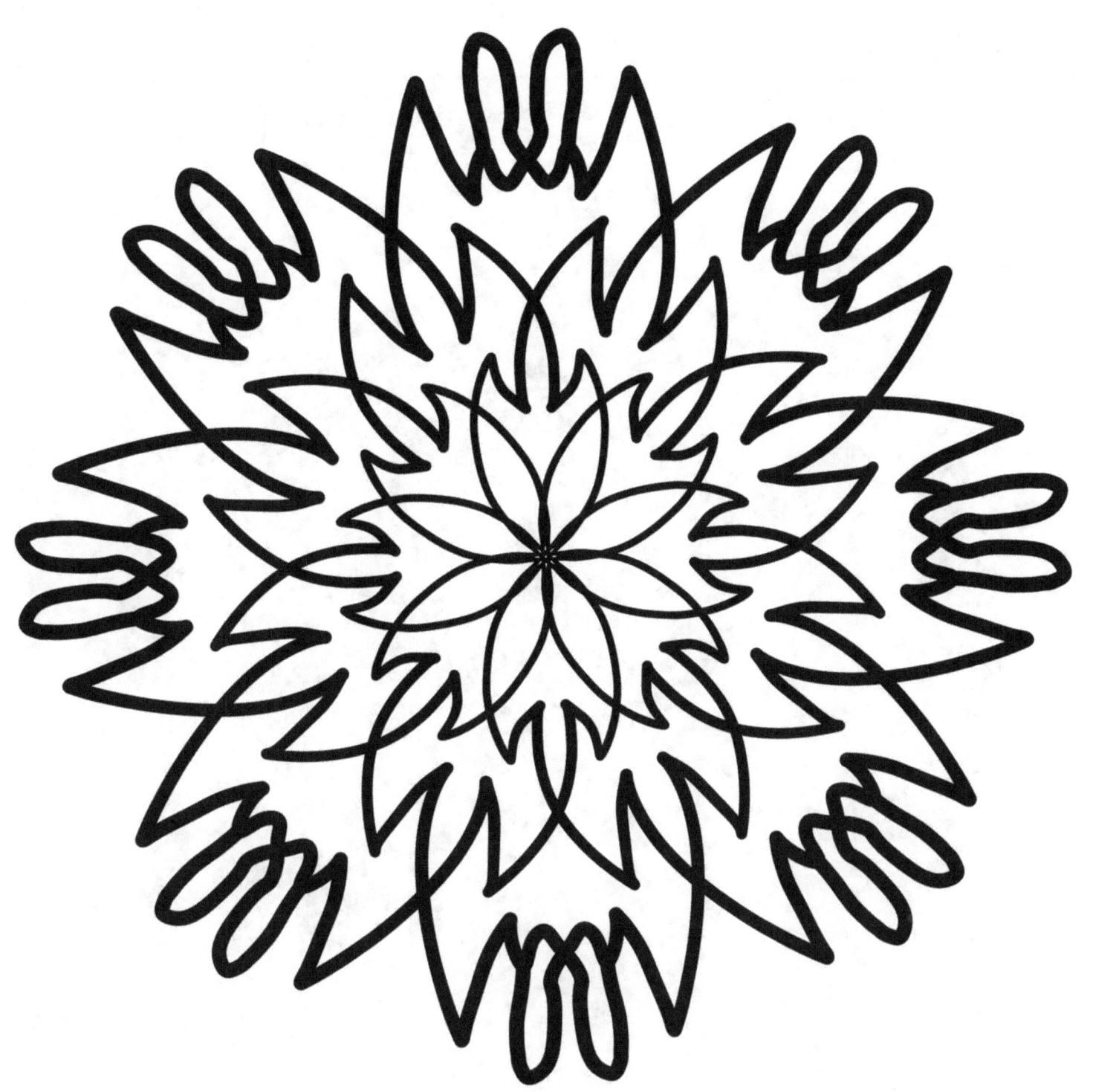

A R T I S T

_____
NAME

_____
DATE

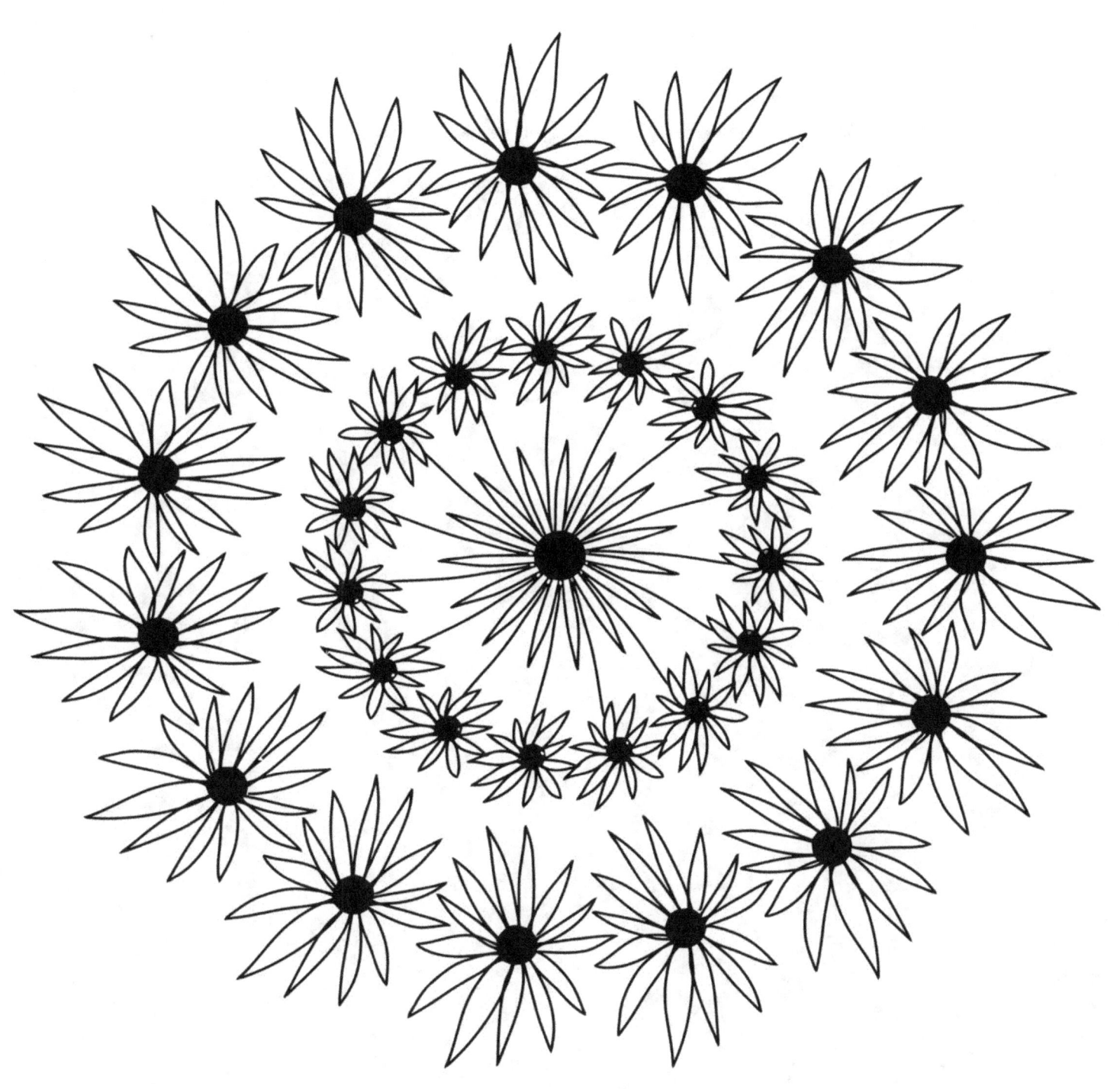

ARTIST

_____

NAME

_____

DATE

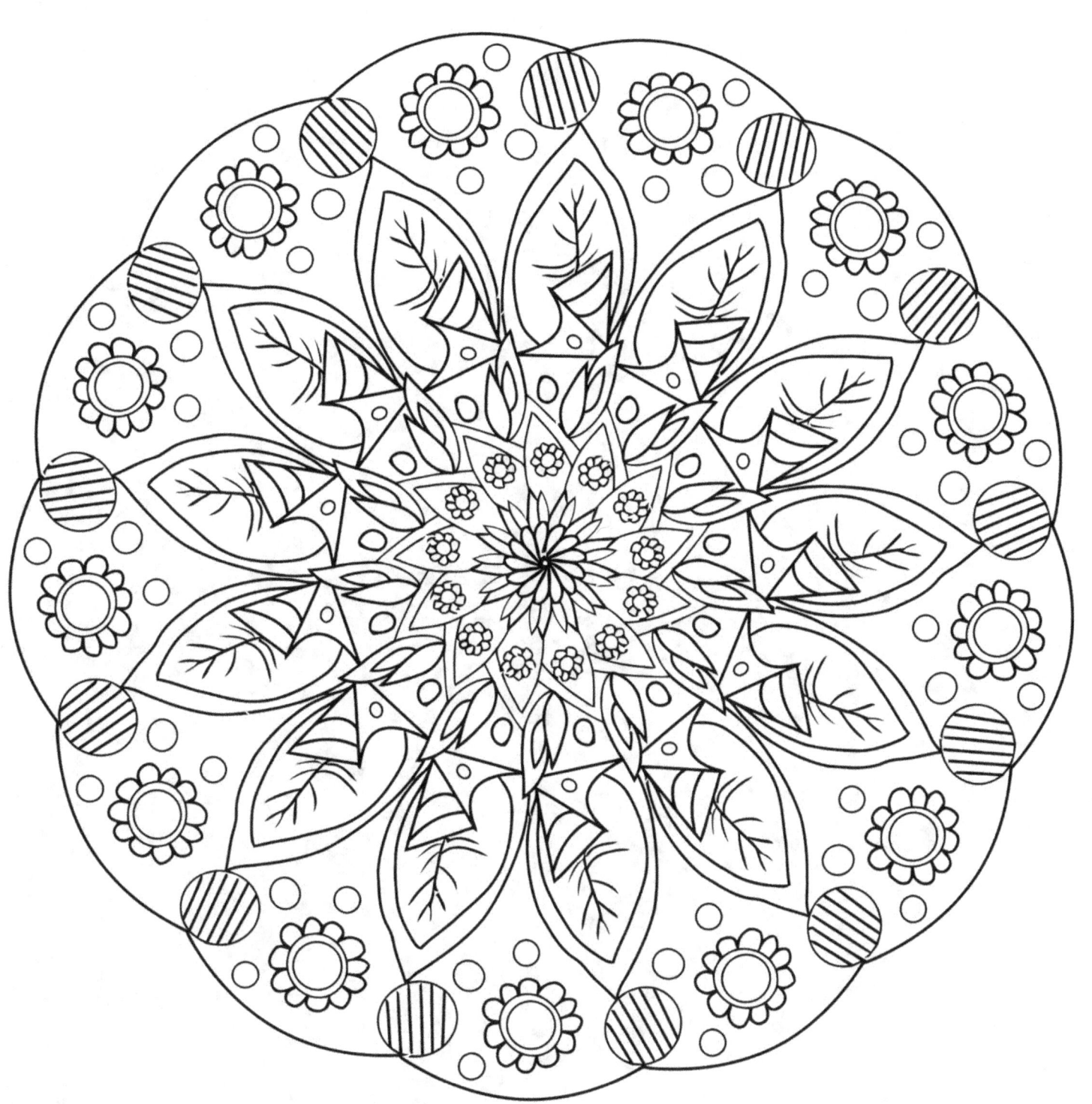

ARTIST

_____
NAME

_____
DATE

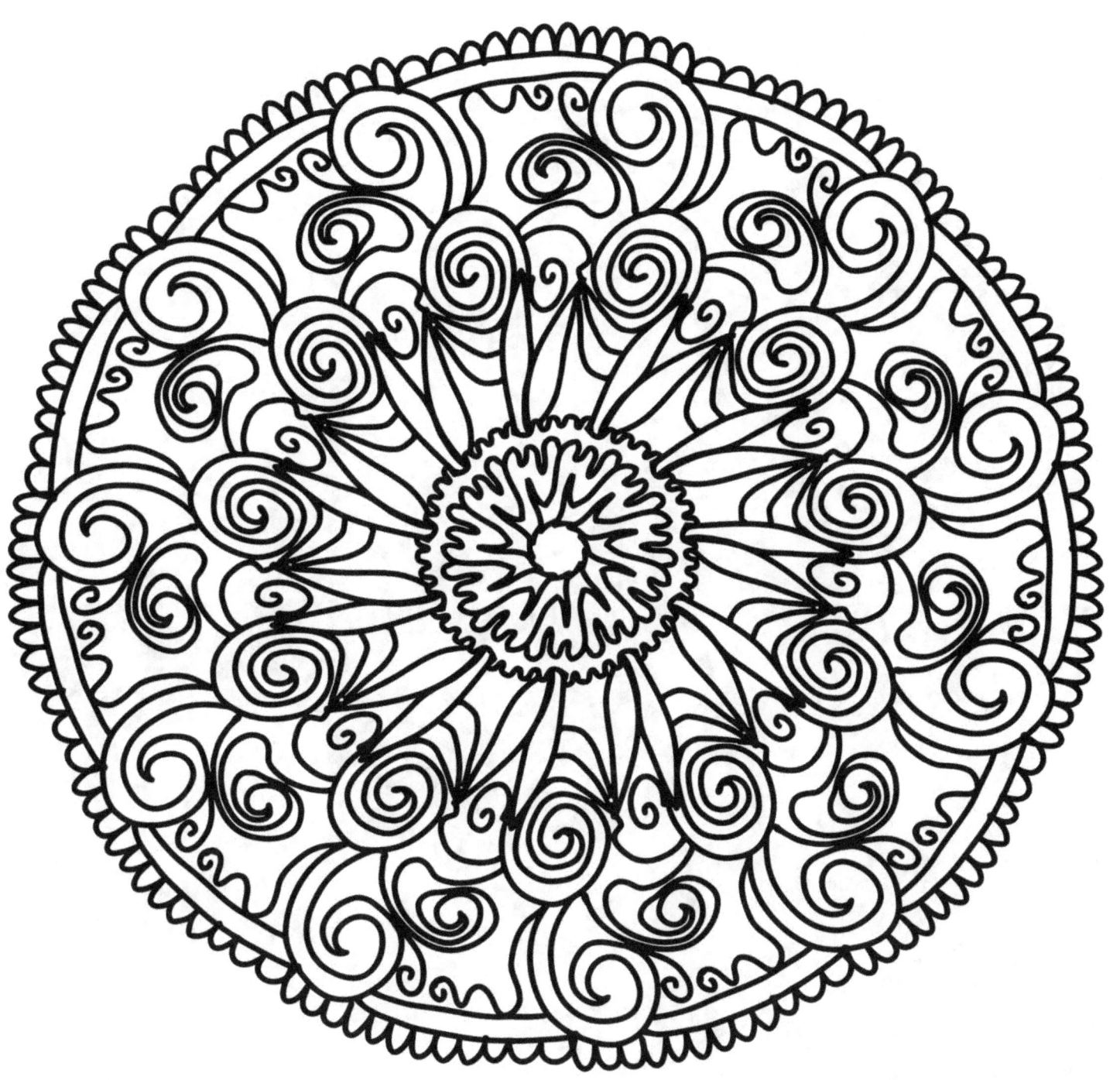

A R T I S T

_____

NAME

_____

DATE

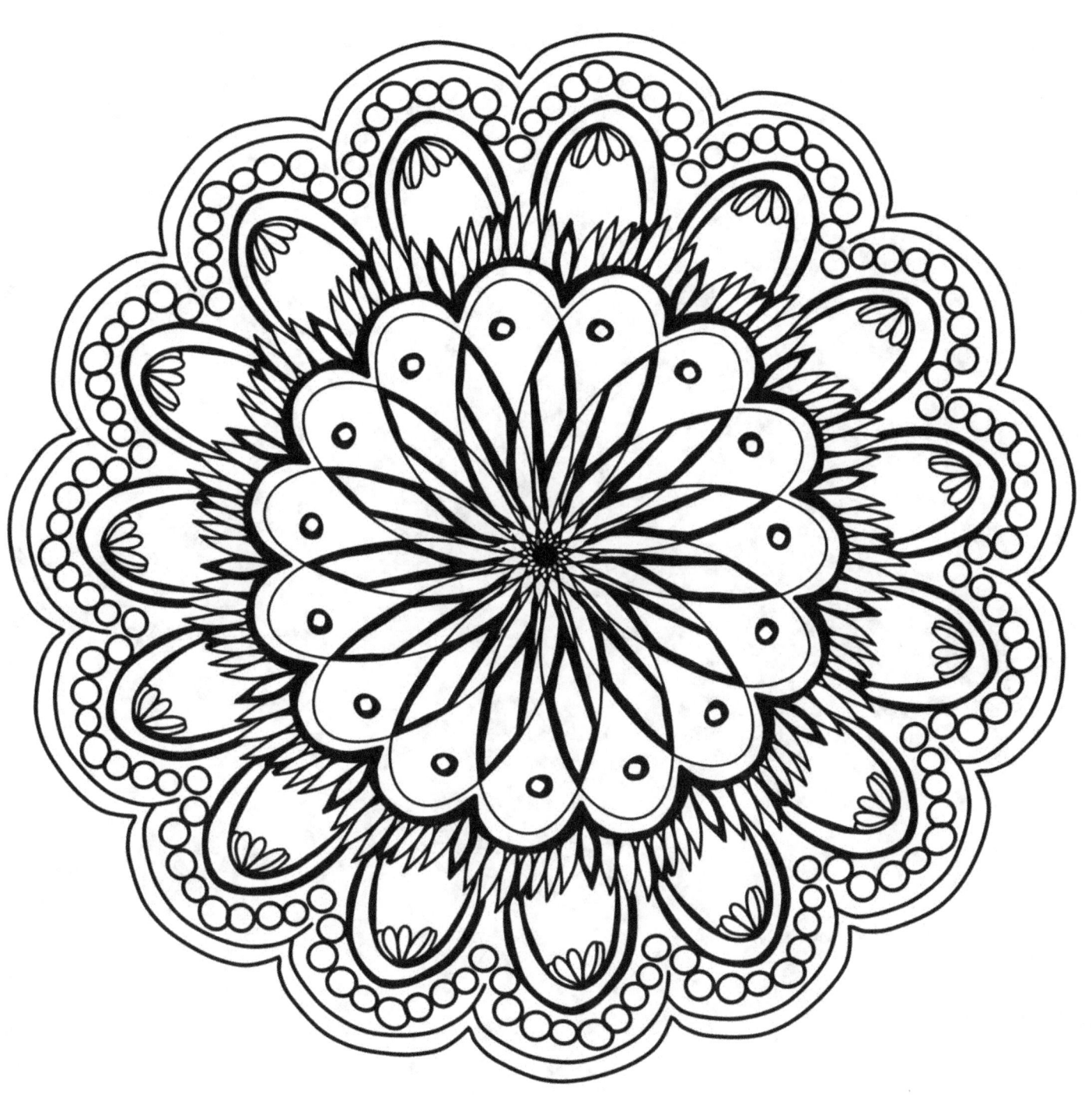

A R T I S T

_____

NAME

_____

DATE

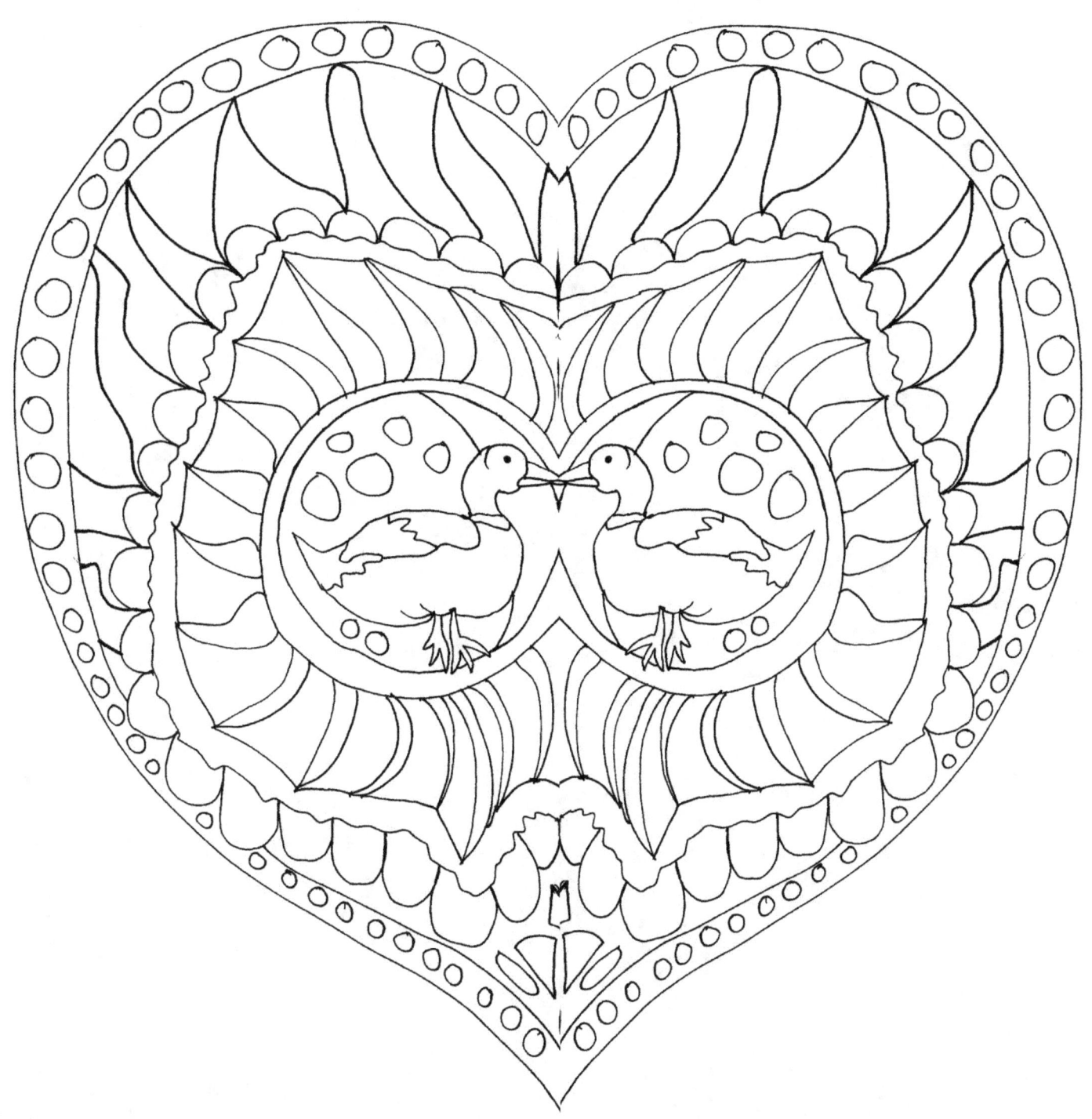

ARTIST

_____
NAME

_____
DATE

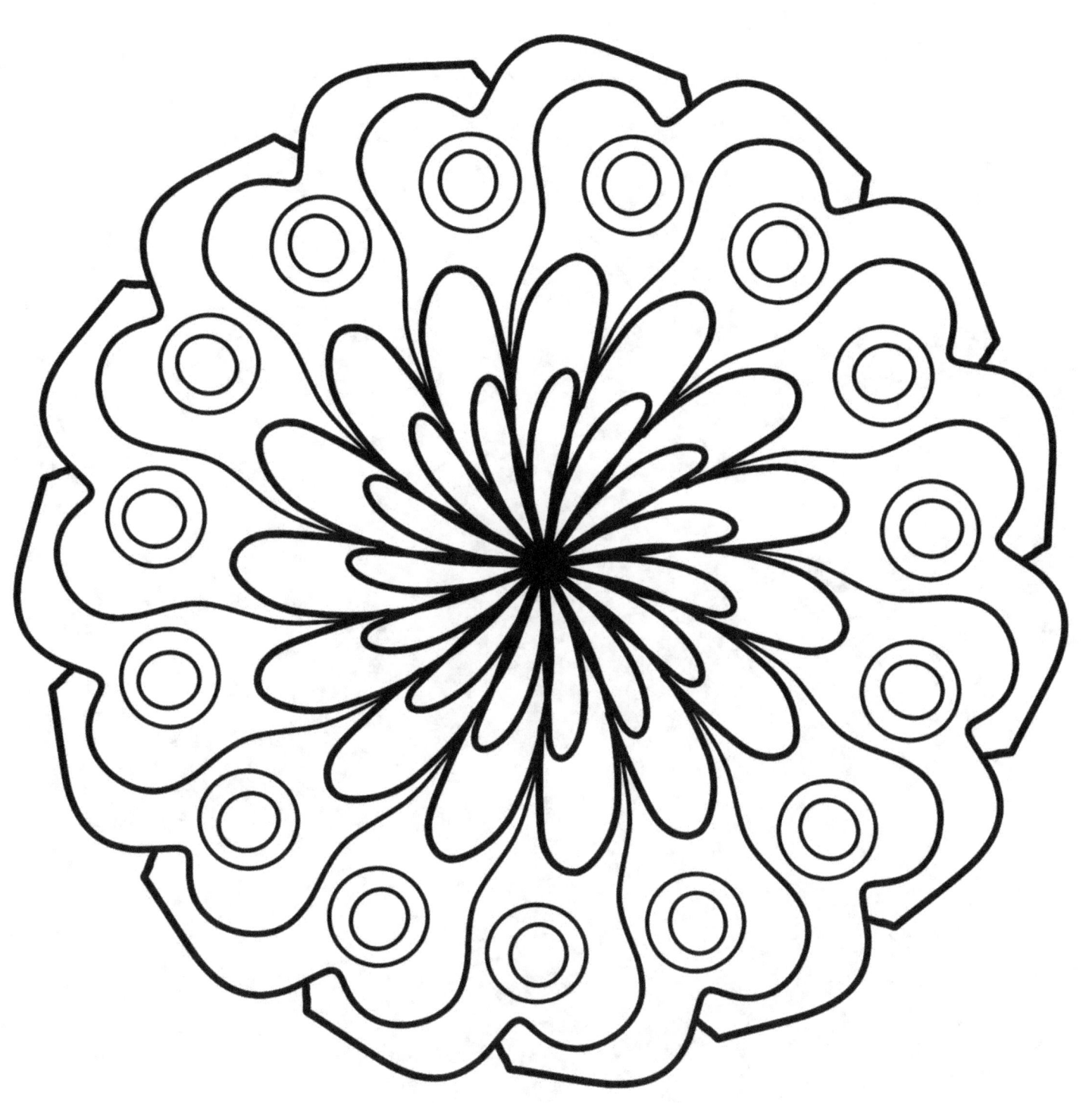

A R T I S T

_____

NAME

_____

DATE

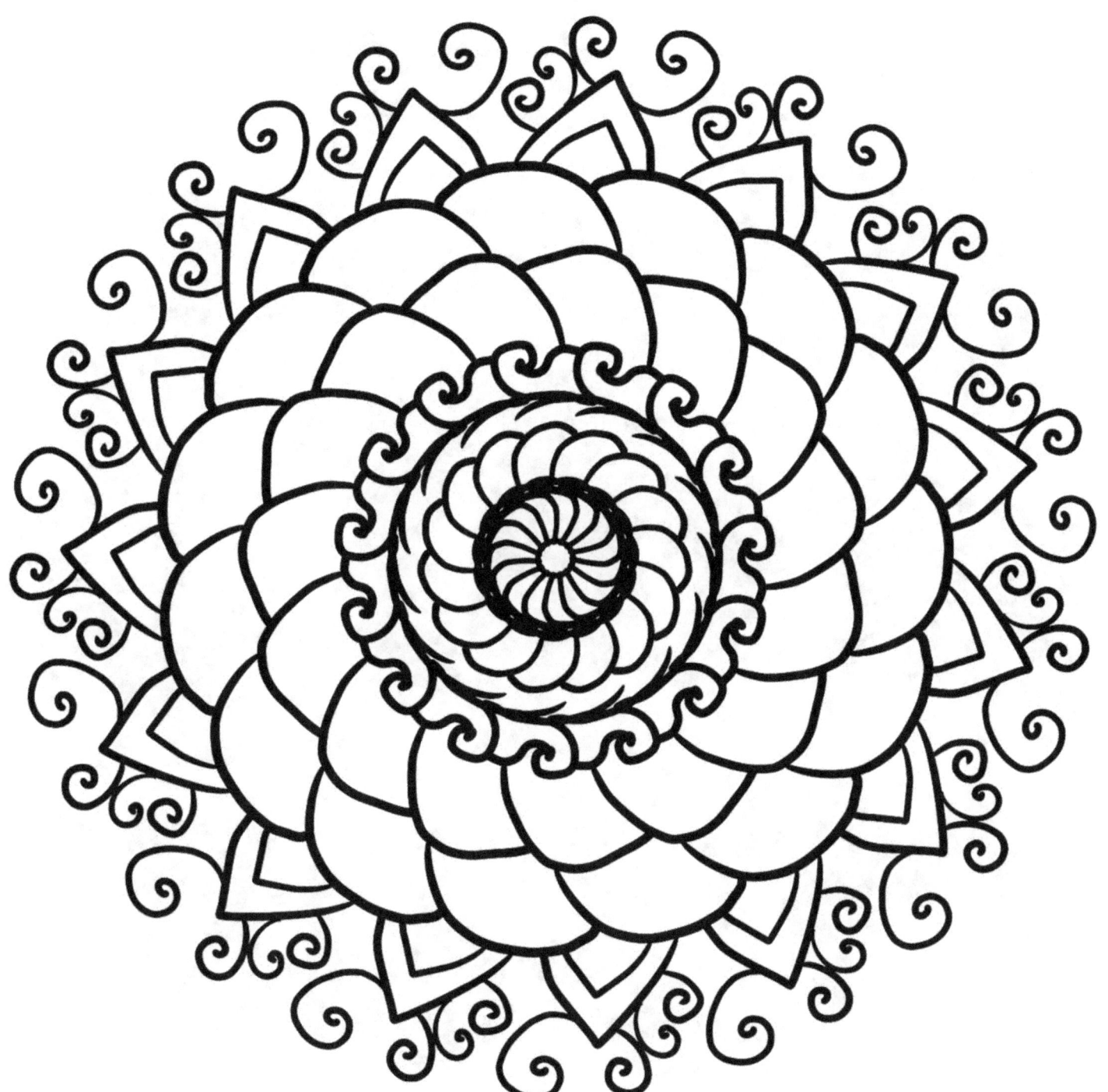

ARTIST

_____

NAME

_____

DATE

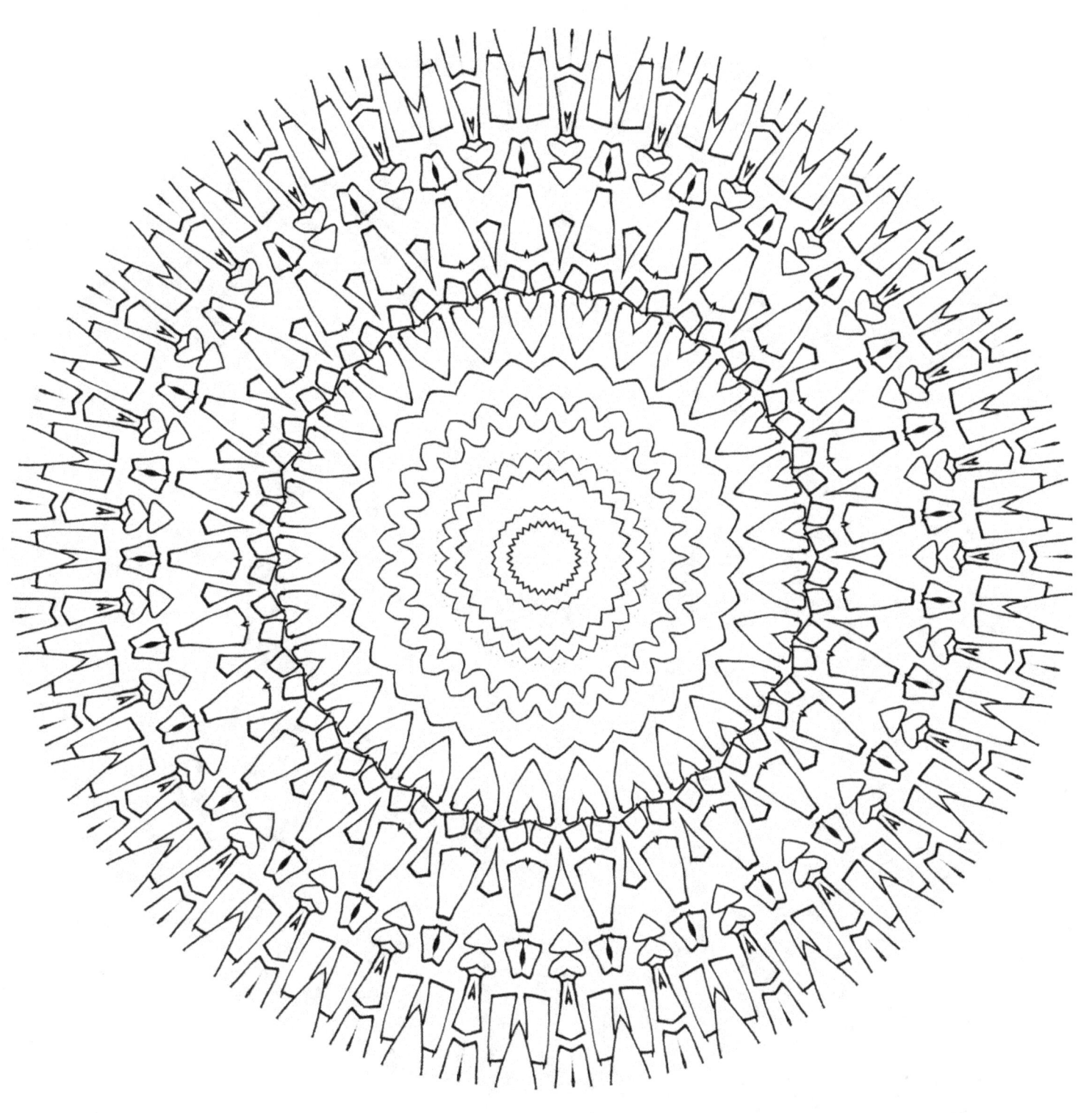

ARTIST

_____
NAME

_____
DATE

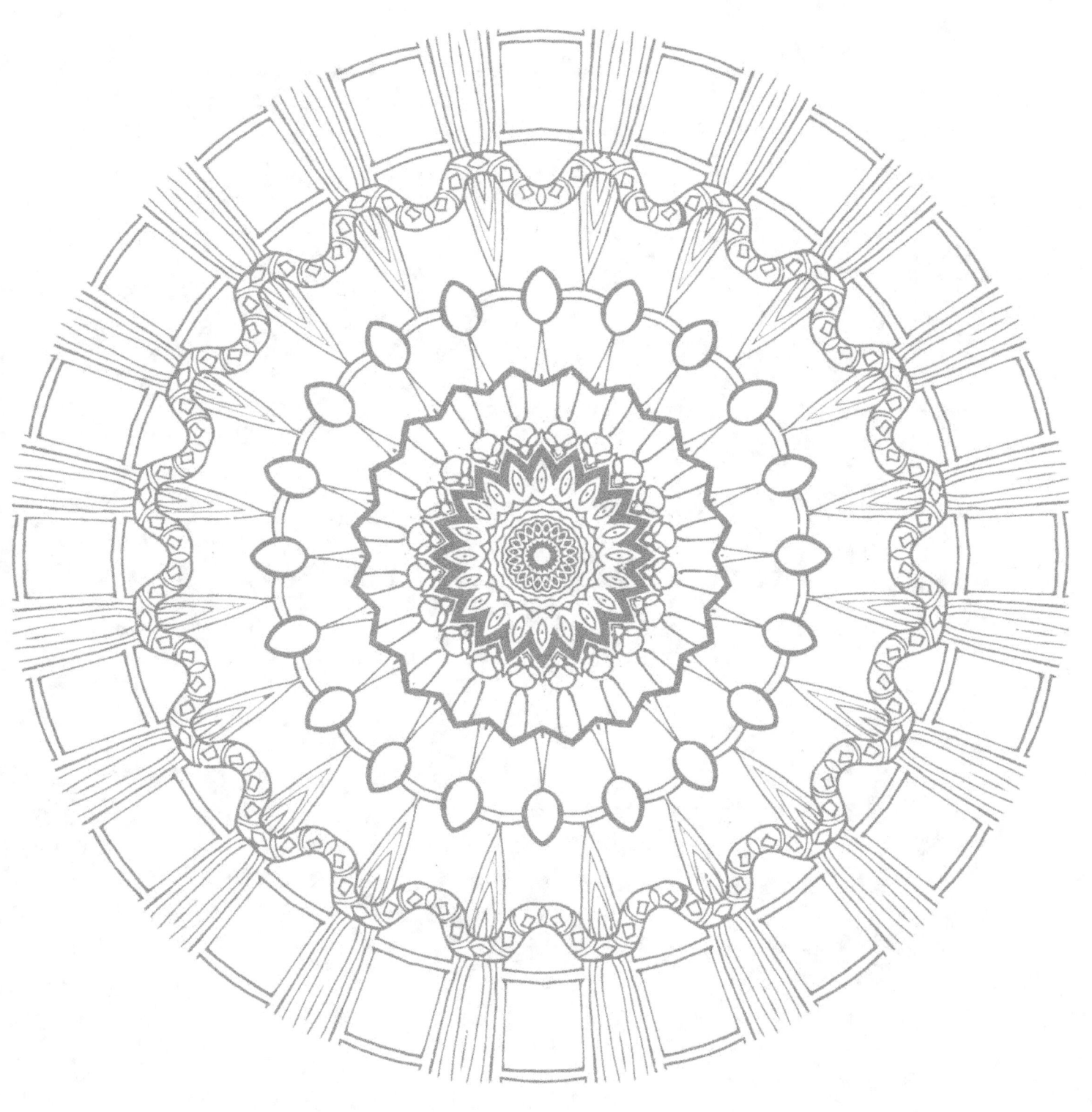

ARTIST

_____
NAME

_____
DATE

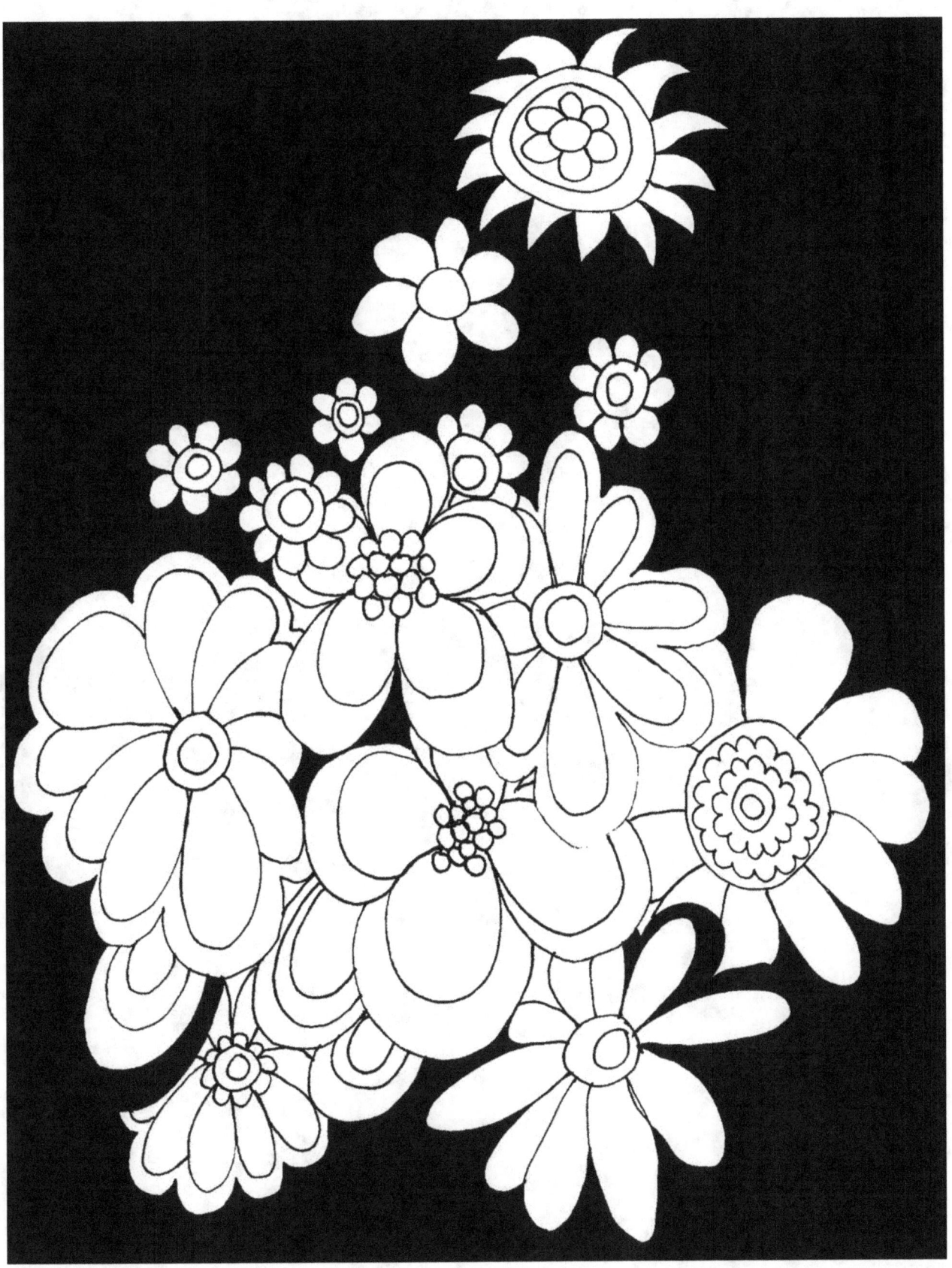

ARTIST

_____

NAME

_____

DATE

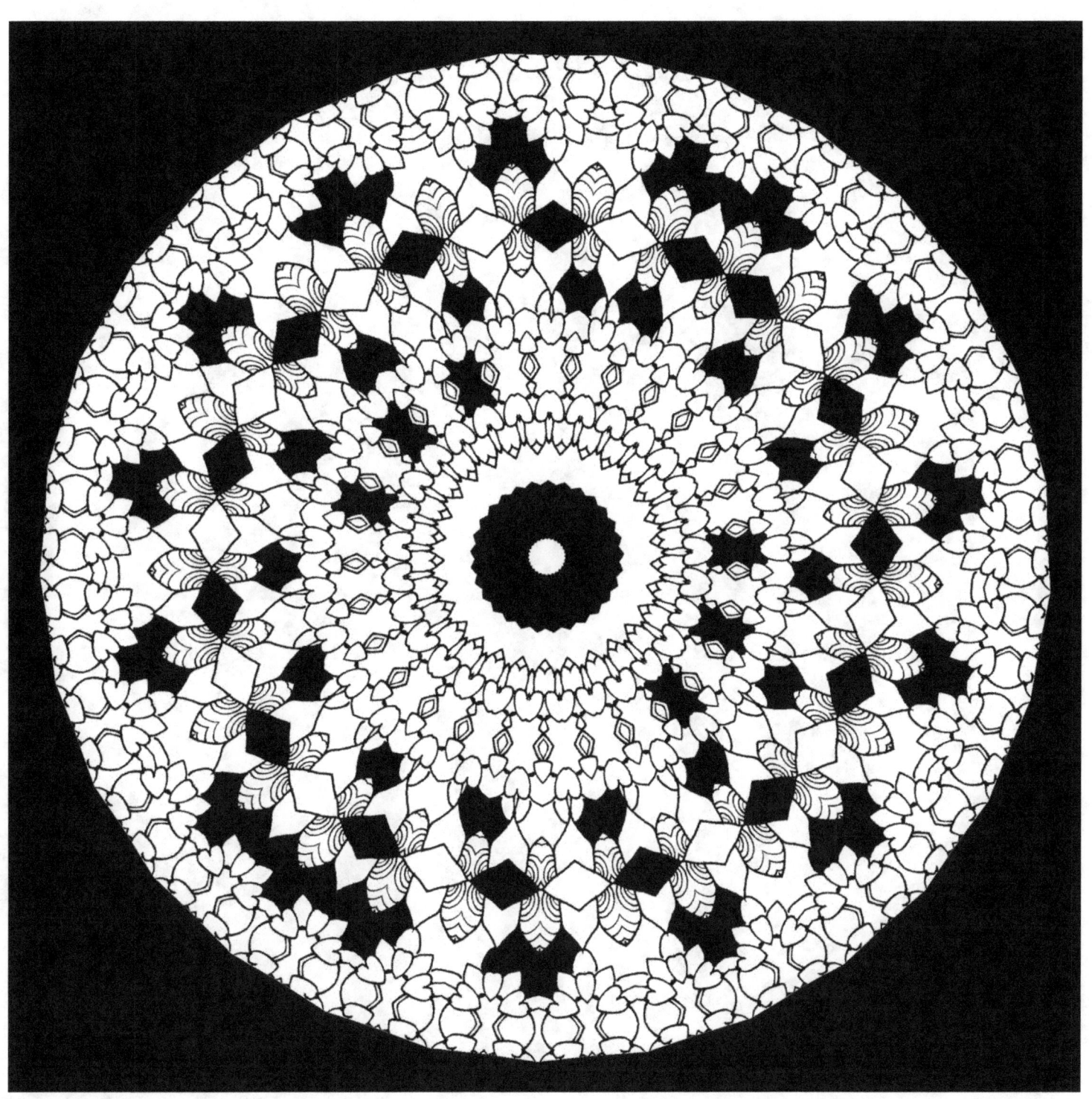

ARTIST

_____
NAME

_____
DATE

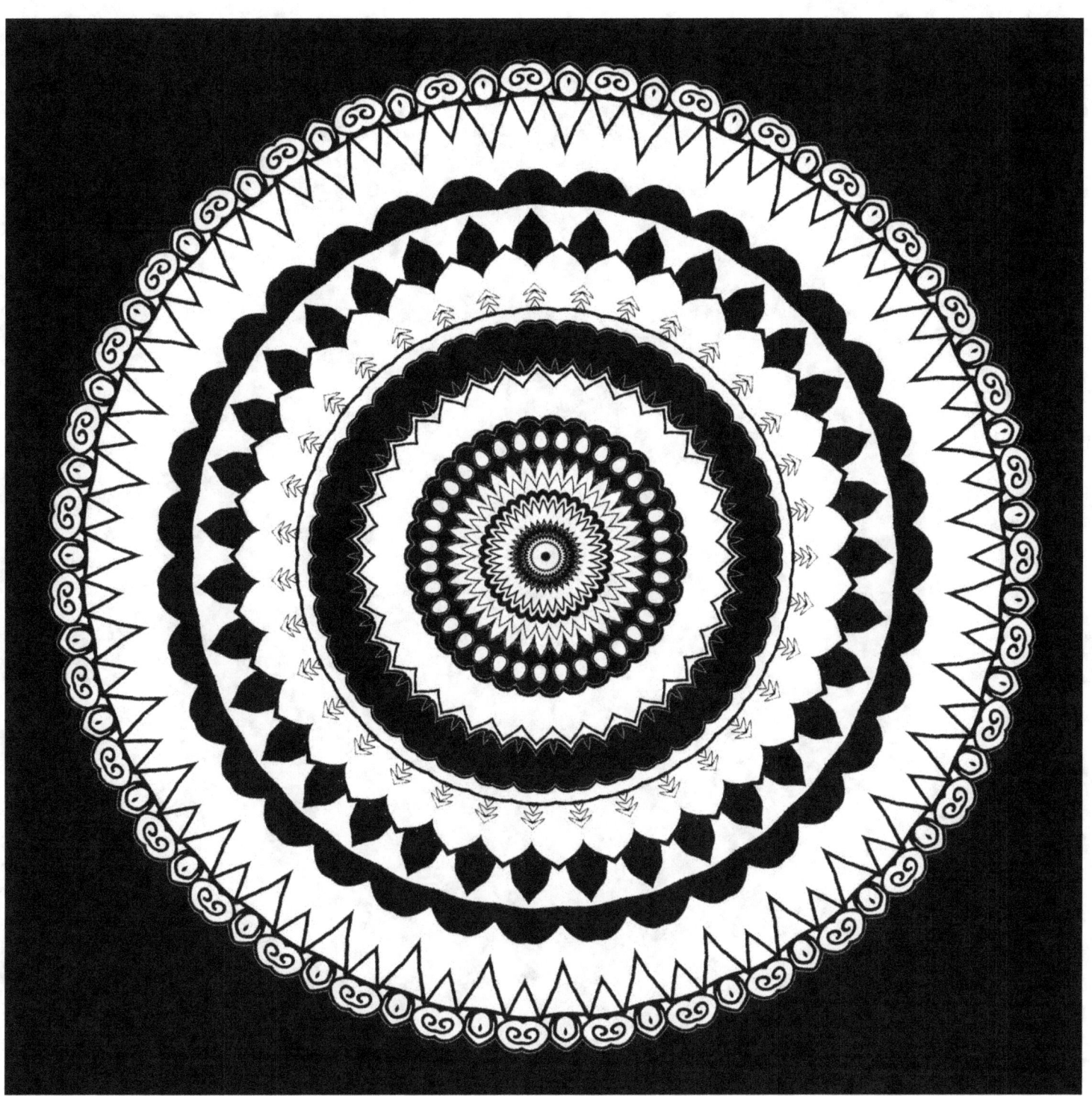

ARTIST

_____
NAME

_____
DATE

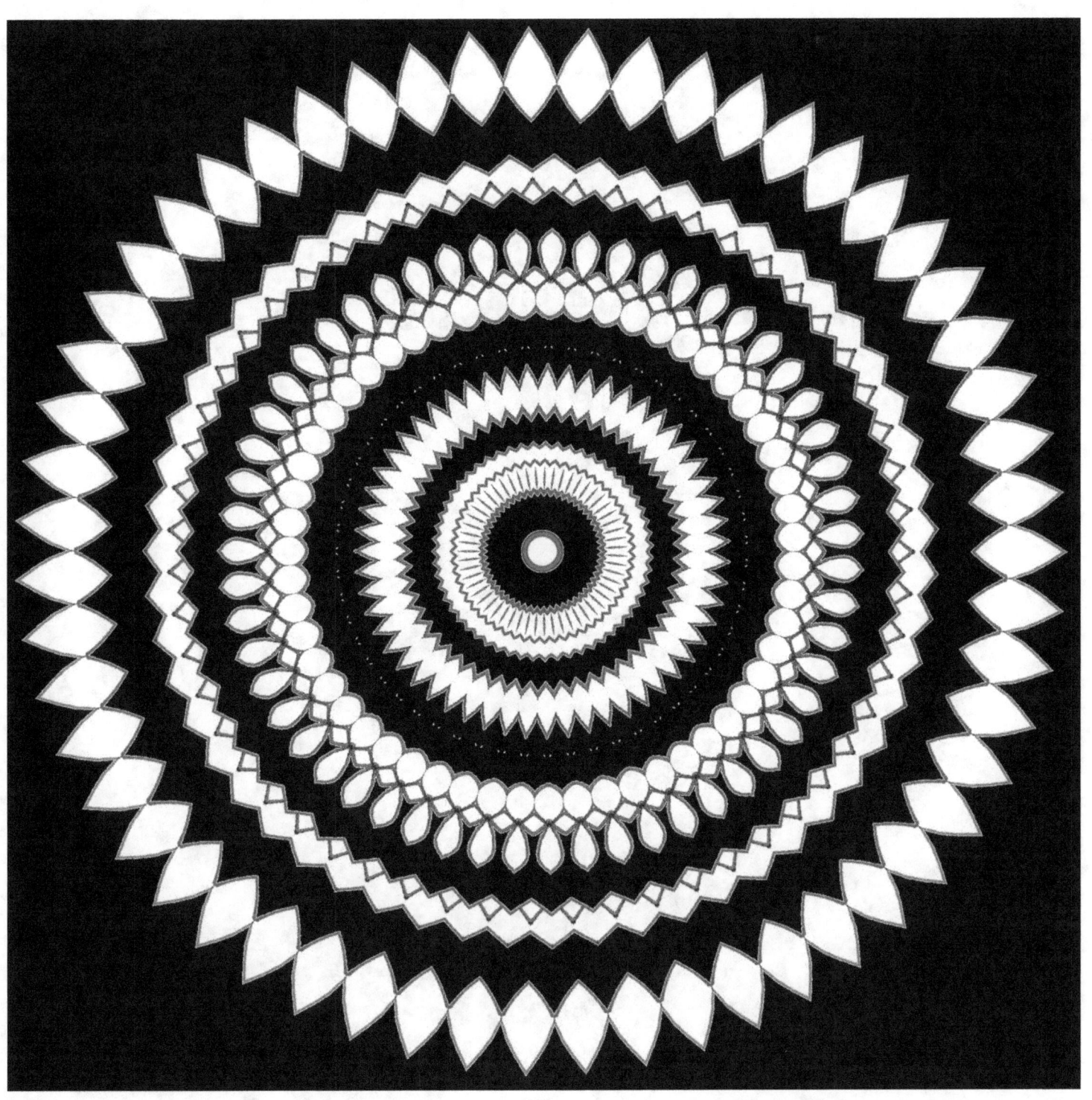

ARTIST

_____

NAME

_____

DATE

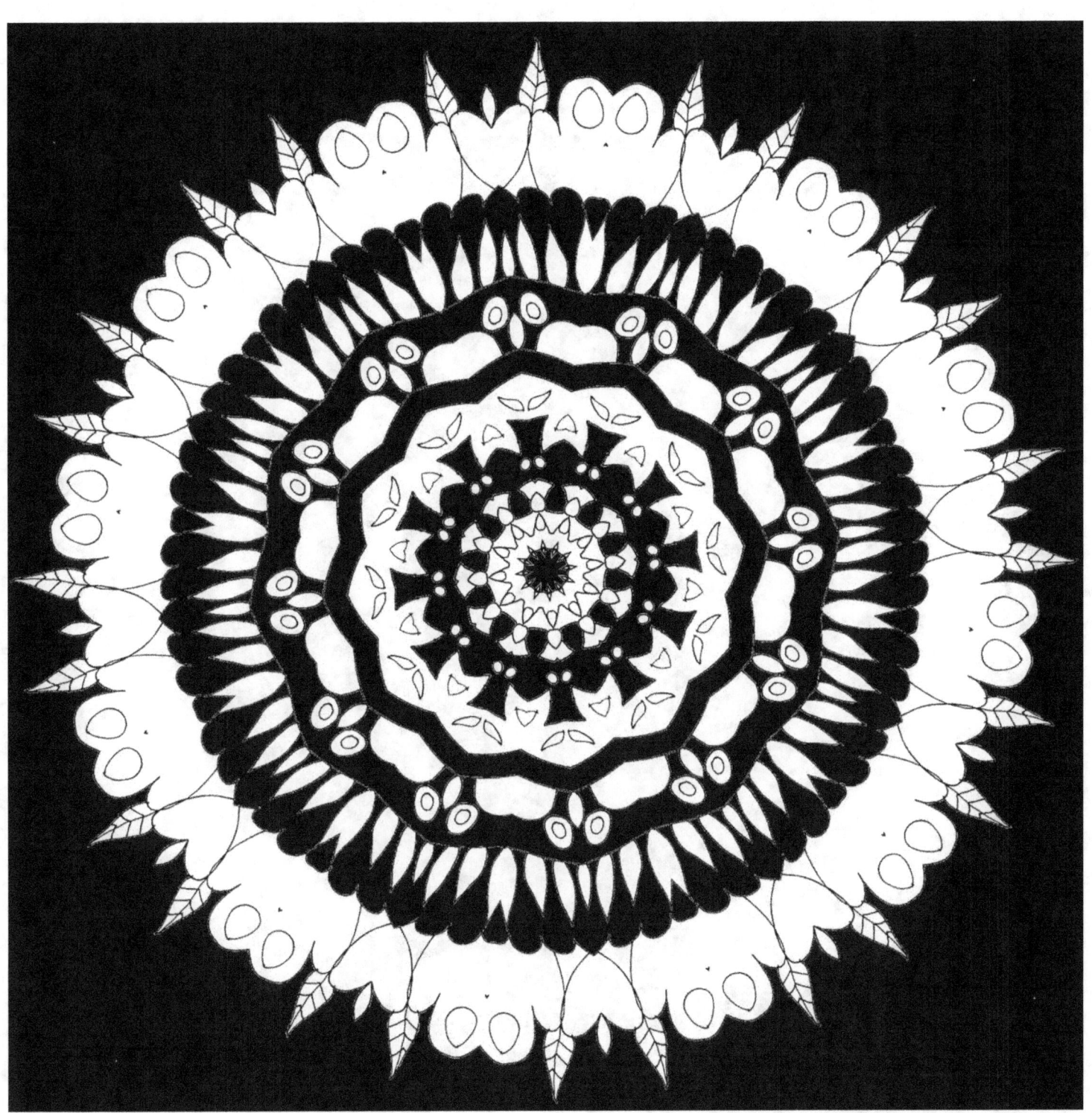

ARTIST

_____
NAME

_____
DATE

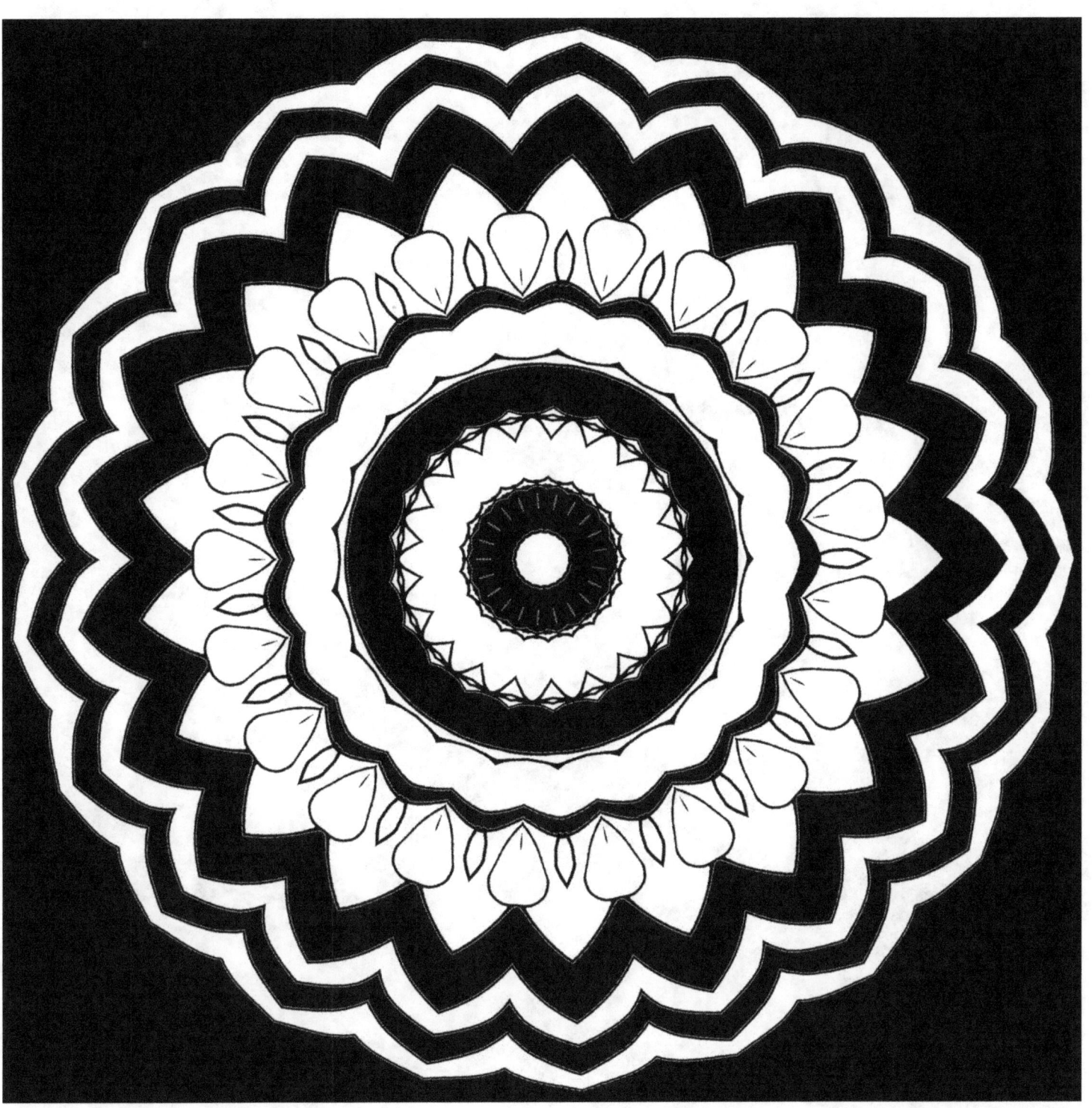

A R T I S T

_____
NAME

_____
DATE

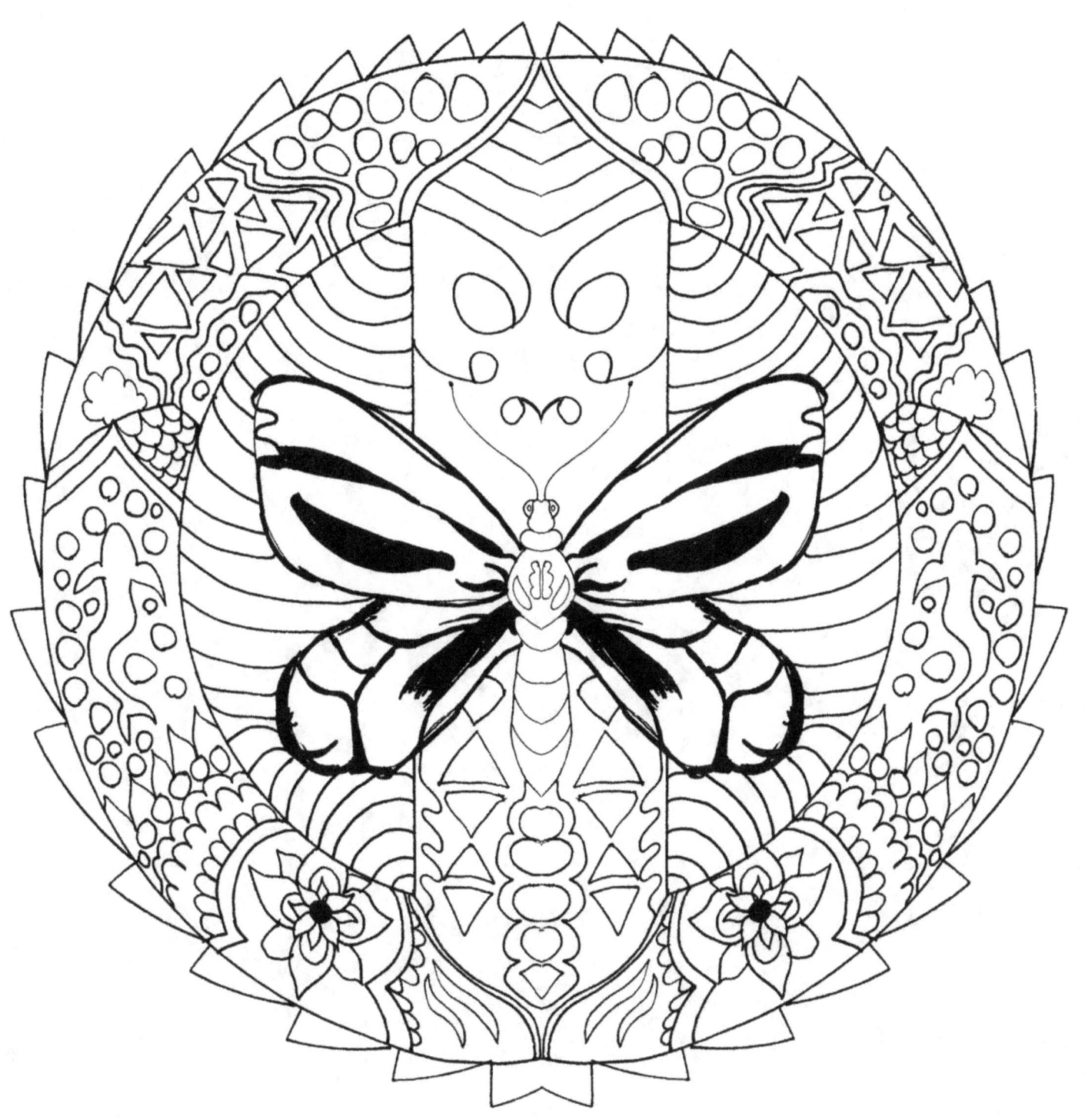

ARTIST

_____
NAME

_____
DATE

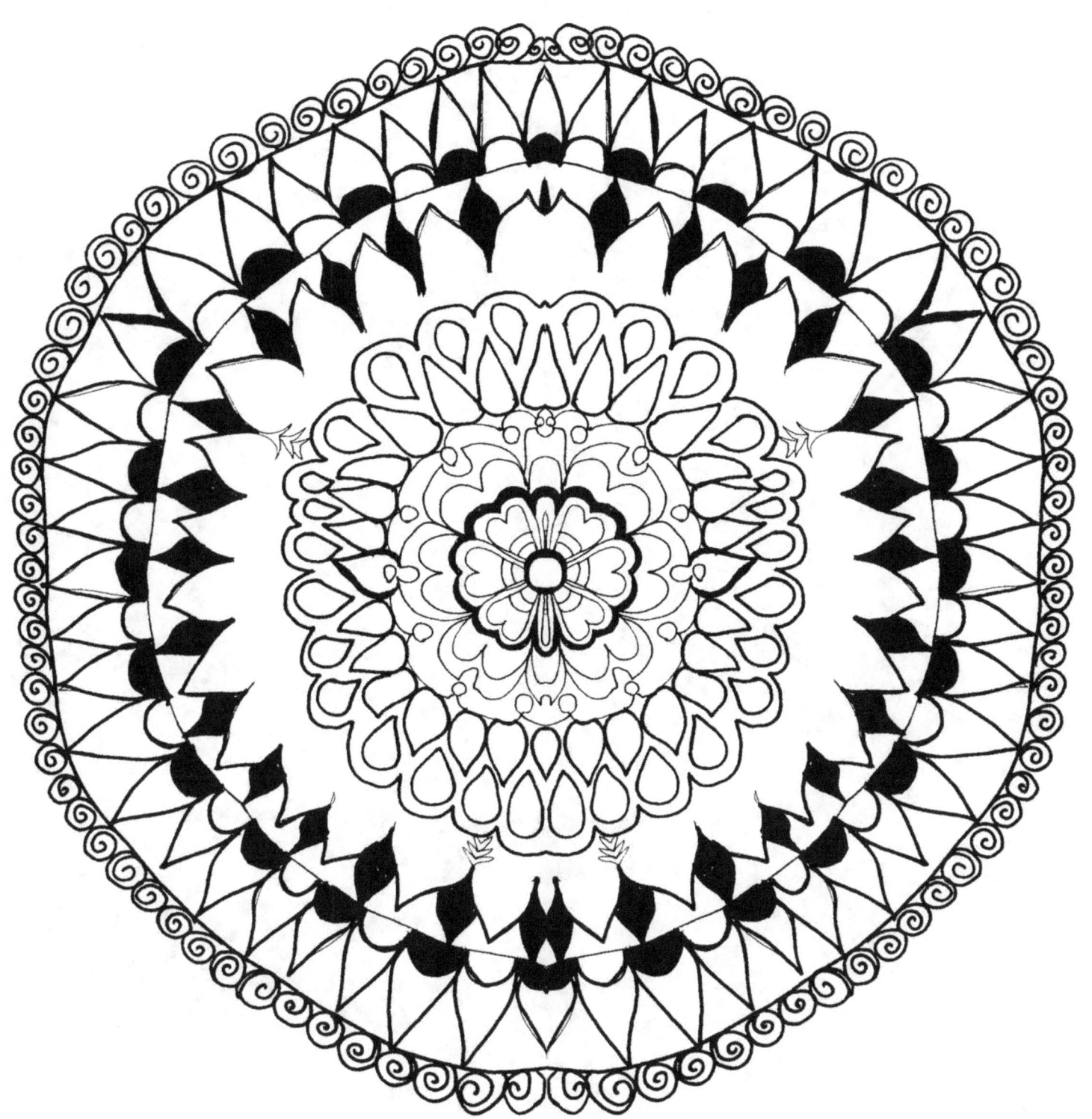

ARTIST

_____
NAME

_____
DATE

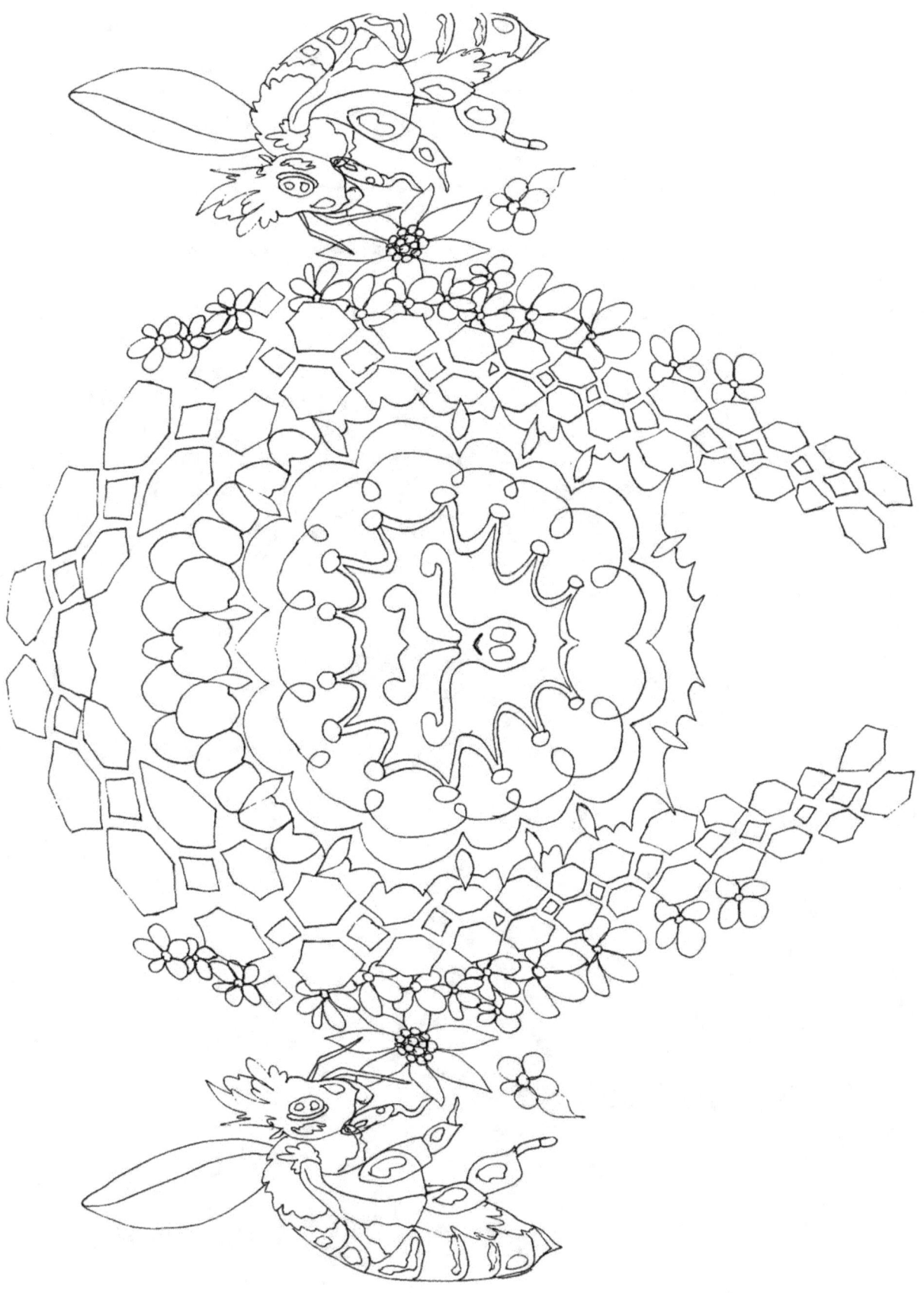

A R T I S T

_____

NAME

_____

DATE

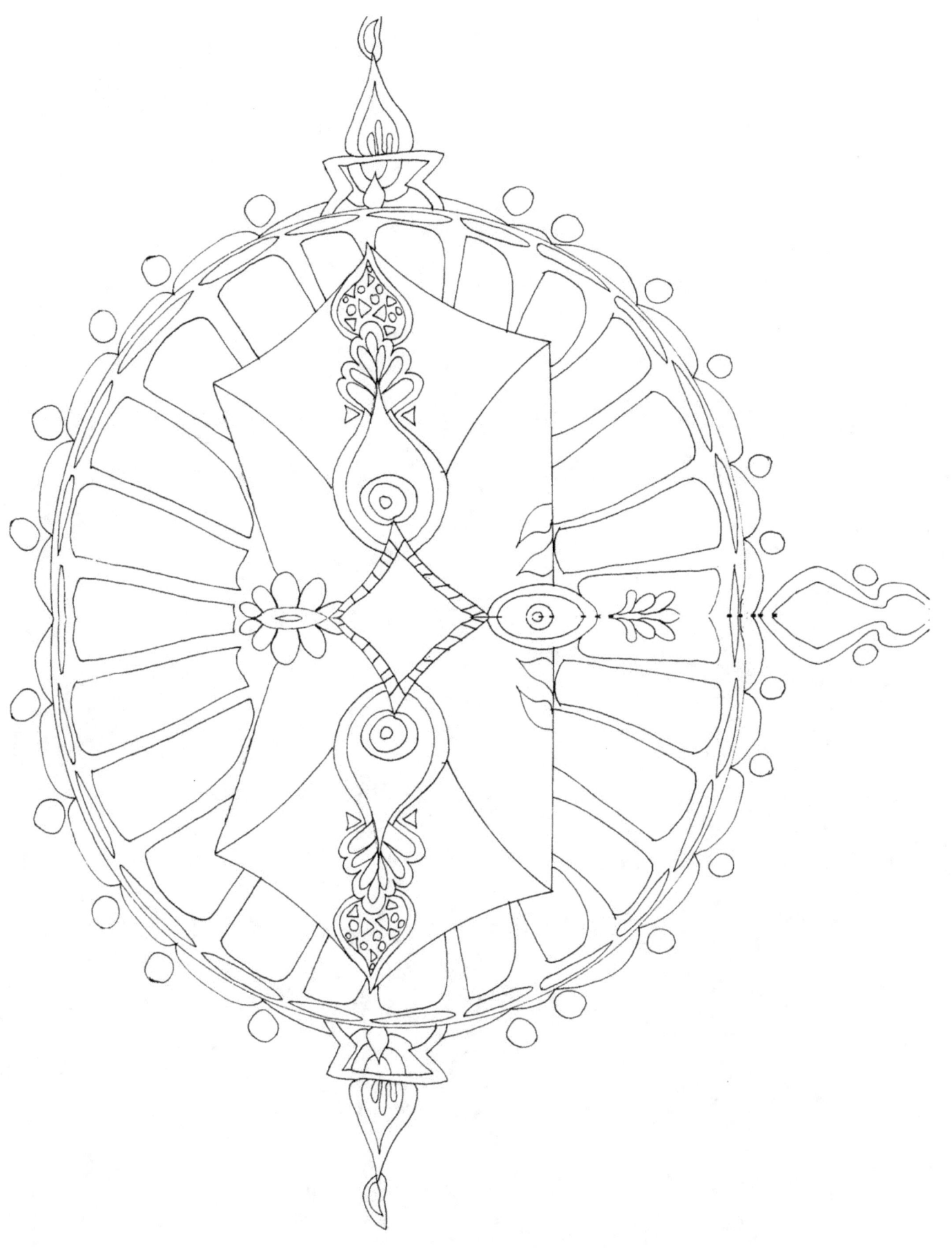

ARTIST

_____
NAME

_____
DATE

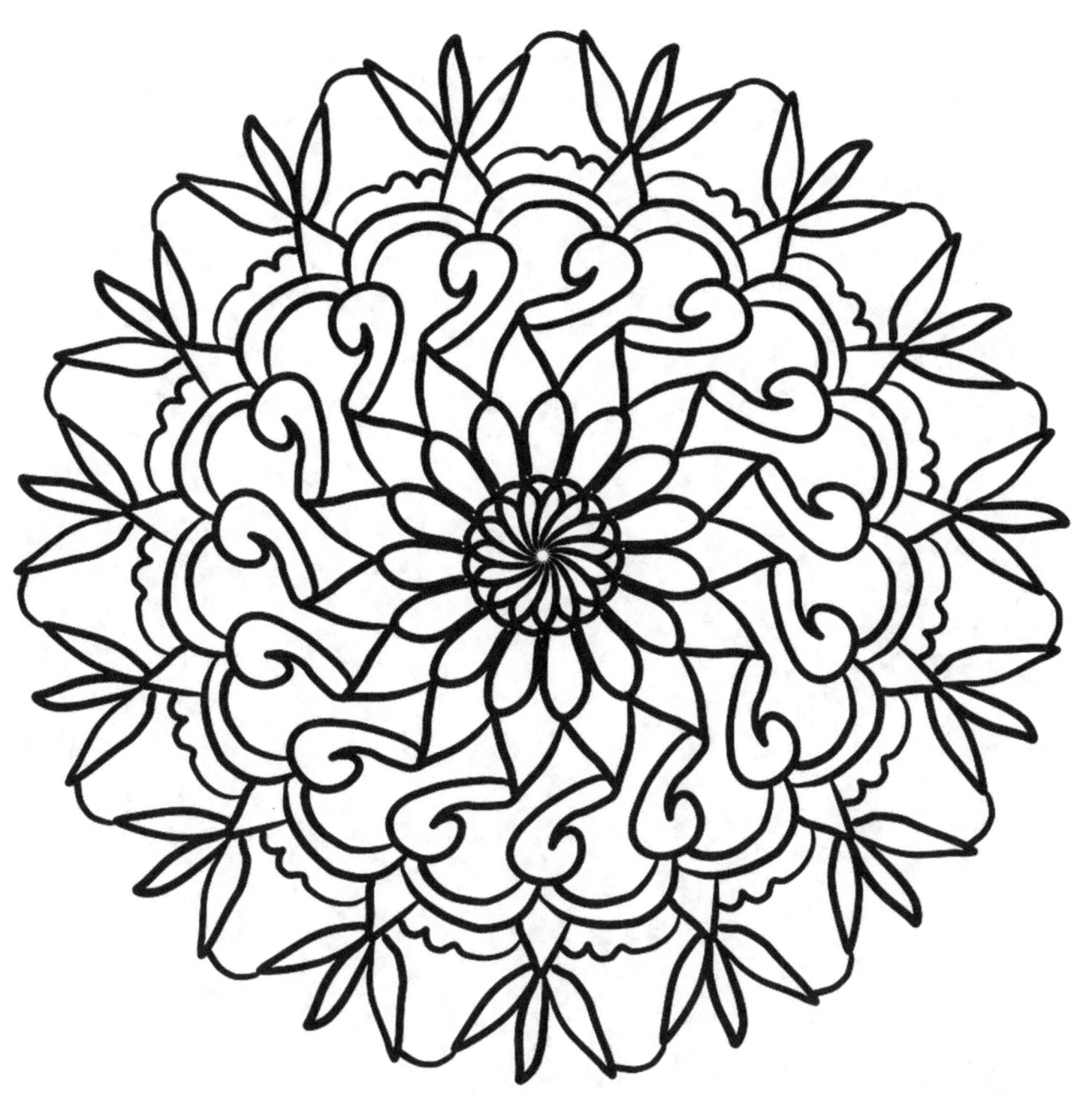

ARTIST

_____
NAME

_____
DATE

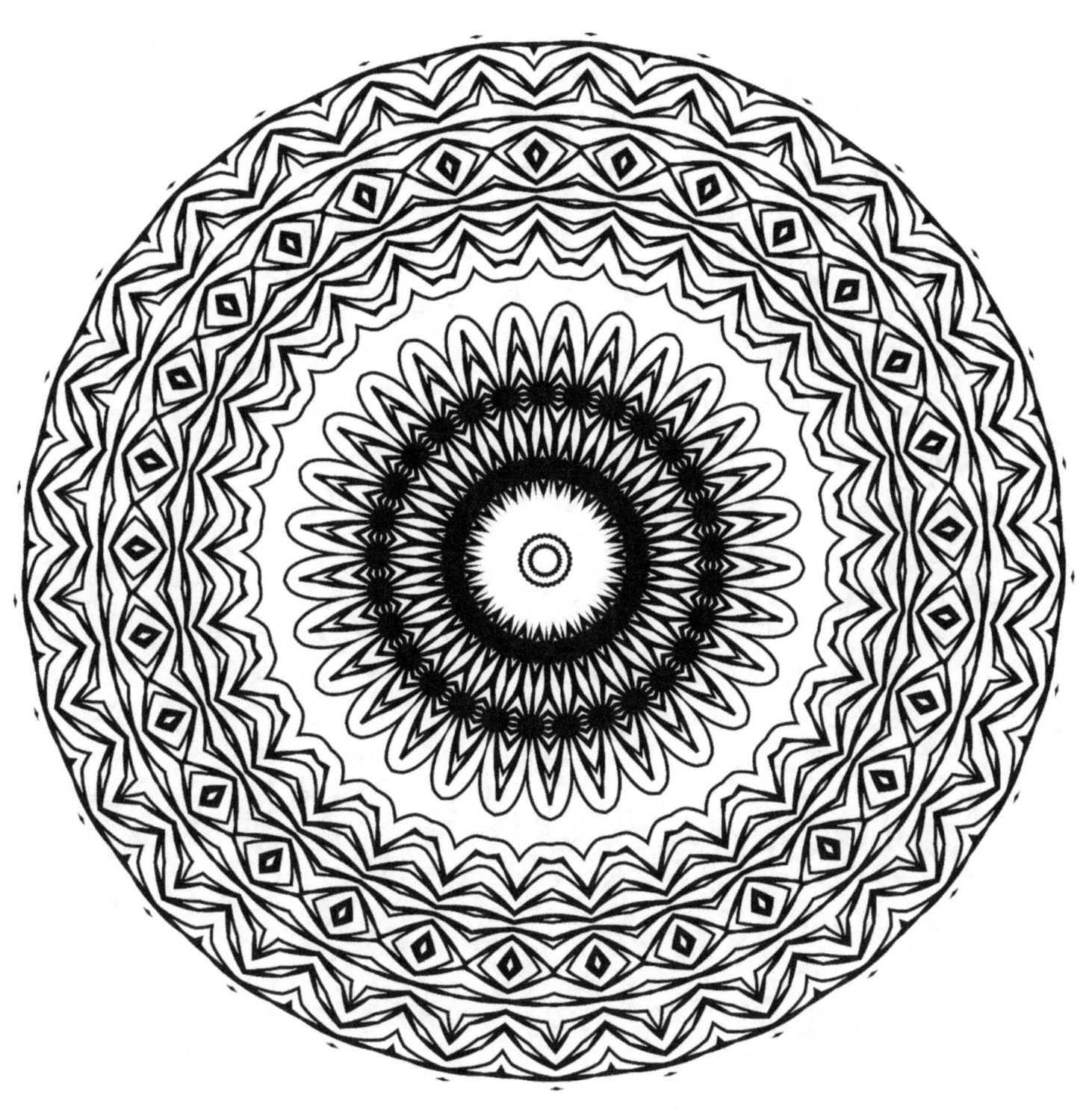

ARTIST

NAME

DATE

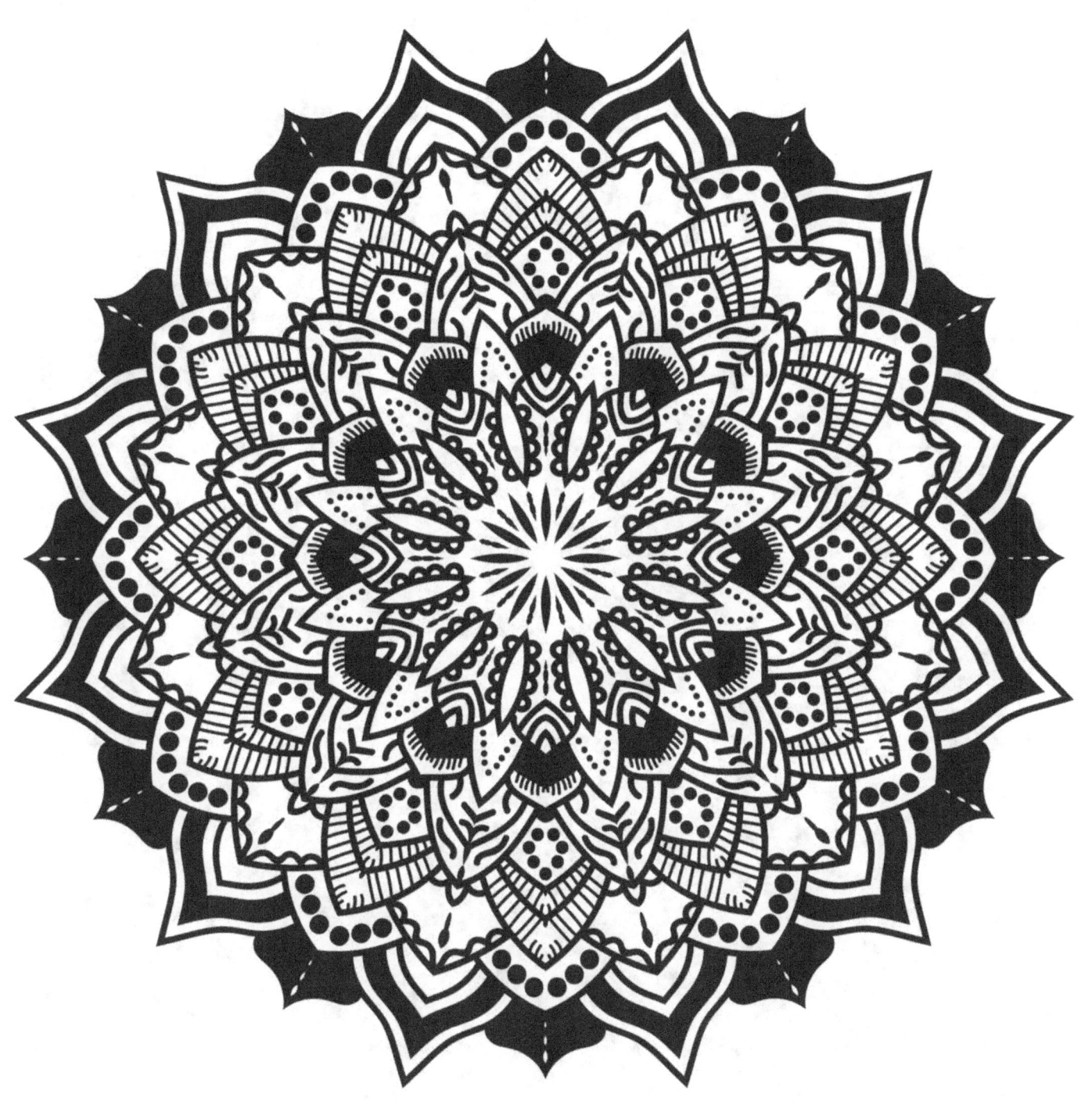

A R T I S T

_____

NAME

_____

DATE

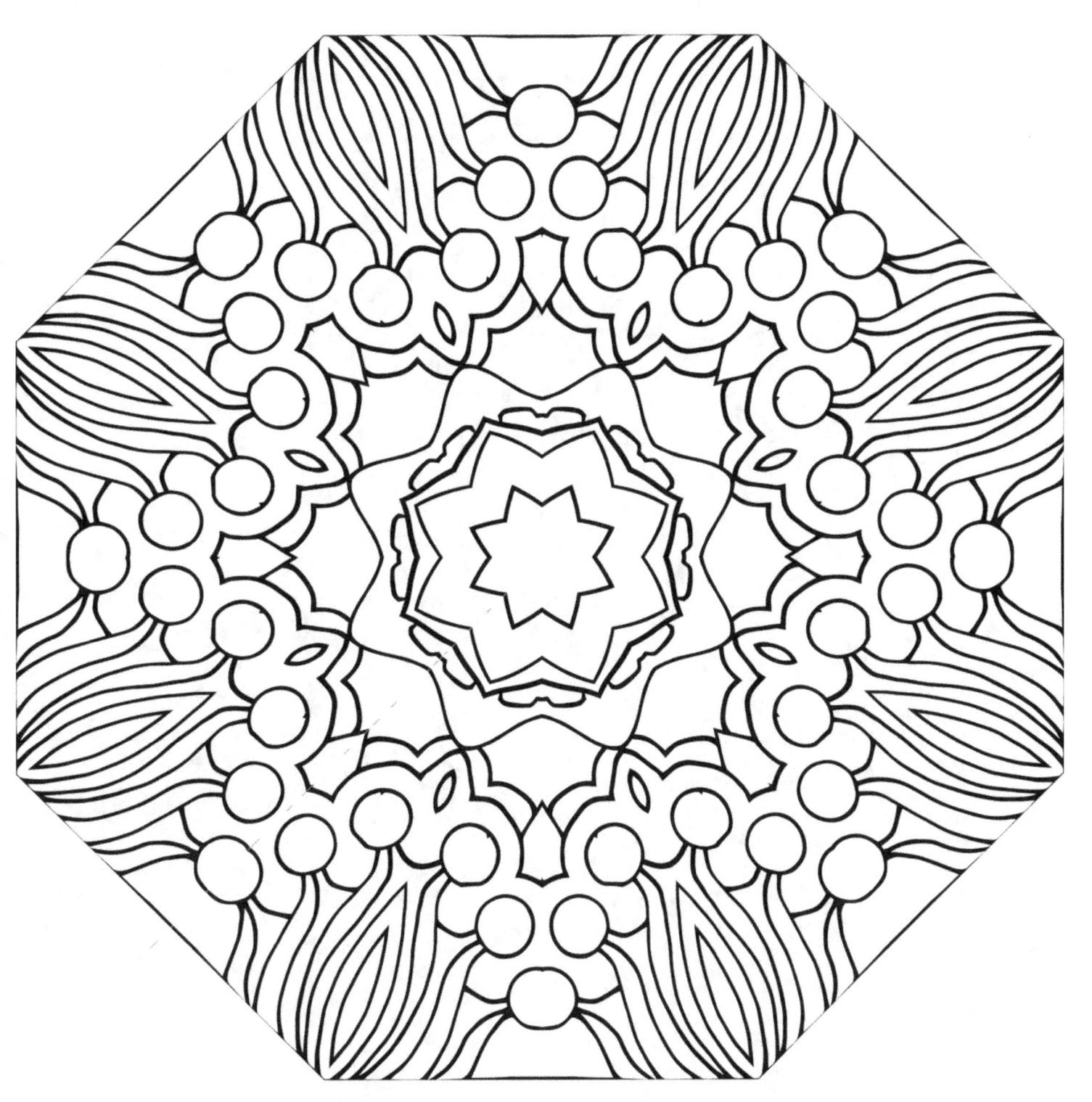

A R T I S T

_____
NAME

_____
DATE

Artist Notes

Other Products

Please visit Jasmines author page for other coloring book titles.

www.amazon.com/author/jasminetaylor (https://goo.gl/AYQdxw)

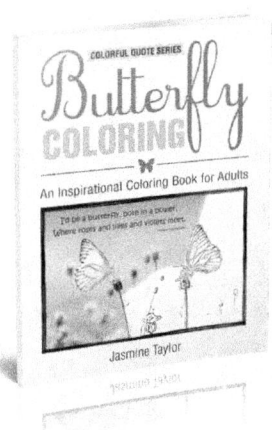
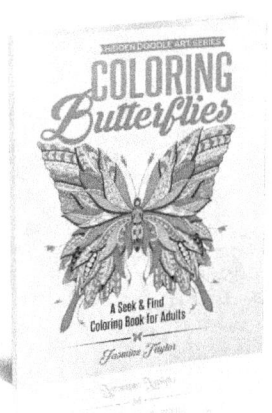
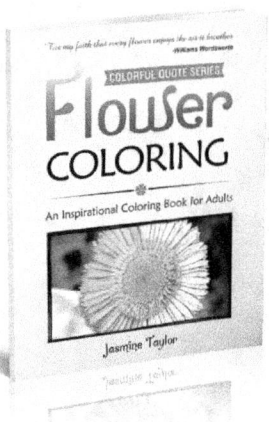

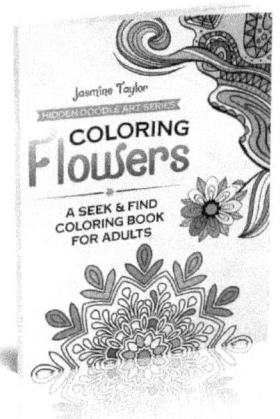
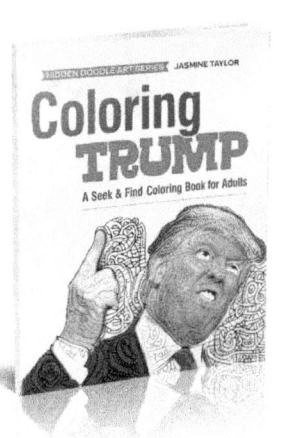
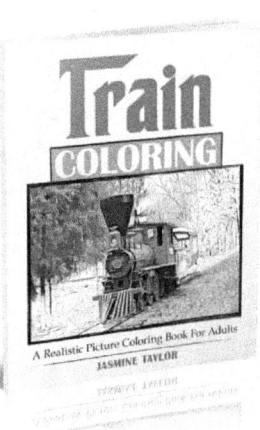

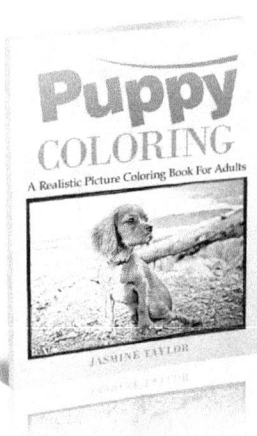
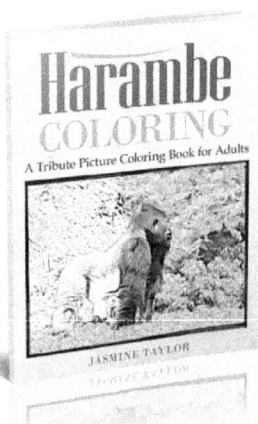
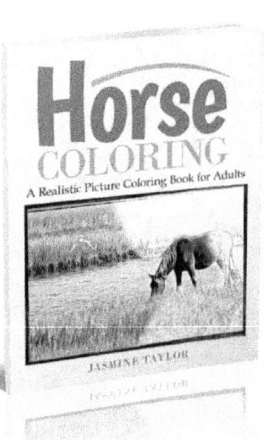

About the Author

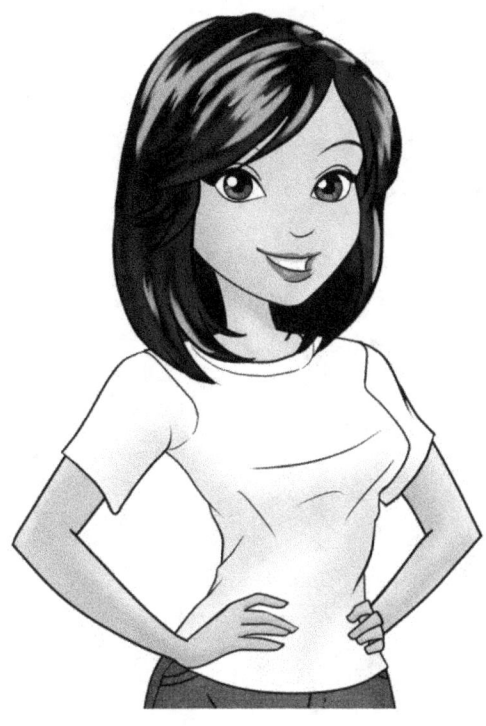

I'm passionate about art, coloring and creativity. My coloring books cover a variety of niches with varying styles and levels of difficulty from beginner to advance for all to enjoy. I'm really thrilled to offer my coloring books to you in the hope of inspiring your creative journey.

If you enjoyed this coloring book, please help others find and benefit as well by leaving a positive review on Lulu or one of its distribution partners. Thank you very much and happy coloring!

Jasmine Taylor

www.ingramcontent.com/pod-product-compliance
Lightning Source LLC
Chambersburg PA
CBHW081248180526
45170CB00007B/2344